Teaching Composition
with Literature

Writing Exercises and Ideas

Teaching Composition with Literature

Writing Exercises and Ideas

Edited by
Dana Gioia

A Special Supplement to accompany
LITERATURE: An Introduction to Fiction, Poetry, and Drama,
Sixth Edition

Teaching Composition with Literature: Writing Exercises and Ideas
edited by Dana Gioia.

Copyright © 1995 HarperCollins College Publishers

ISBN: 0-673-54274-2

95 96 97 98 99   9 8 7 6 5 4 3 2 1

Contents

~~~~~~

WRITING ASSIGNMENTS ON STORIES

Poetry

GENERAL WRITING ASSIGNMENTS

WRITING ASSIGNMENTS ON POEMS

WRITING ASSIGNMENTS ON PLAYS

APPENDIX: A MODEL COURSE OUTLINE

Preface

~~~~~~

The design of *Teaching Composition with Literature* is unabashedly practical. The volume tries to assist instructors who use stories, poems, and plays in teaching expository writing. The volume is designed to accompany *Literature: An Introduction to Fiction, Poetry, and Drama* (Sixth Edition), edited by X. J. Kennedy and me. All of the writing exercises and assignments in *Teaching Composition with Literature* use selections from the current edition of *Literature* as their focus or departure point.

In compiling *Teaching Composition with Literature*, the editor asked a cross-section of excellent English teachers for help. I approached various instructors from all regions of the country with a request for a composition exercise or assignment they had used in the classroom with conspicuous success. In teaching, there is no substitute for practical experience, and the purpose of this book is to share it. Every instructor knows how much one can learn from colleagues who have taught the same or a similar course. We may never be fortunate enough to have the instructors in this volume for colleagues, but this collection will give us the chance to hear and perhaps borrow some of their ideas.

Reading scholarly journals today, one would assume that most college instructors spend their time wrestling with sophisticated theoretical issues. It will come as no surprise to any reader of this book that most teachers face more mundane and pragmatic challenges, especially the never-ending task of teaching undergraduates to write competent expository prose. *Teaching Composition with Literature* is not intended to replace the many excellent books in the field of composition. Rather, it is designed to supplement one of the most popular approaches, which uses imaginative literature as a means for teaching expository writing. This volume gathers together for the first time a representative sampling of proven writing exercises created by instructors for use in their own classrooms.

The inspiration for *Teaching Composition with Literature* came from the experience of assembling the new edition of *Literature: An Introduction to Fiction, Poetry, and Drama*. As part of the editorial process, X. J. Kennedy and I sent out a rough draft of our new table of contents to a cross-section of instructors for review. Their comments helped us to develop the final book. As we read through their reactions, we were impressed by how often instructors argued for a particular story, poem, or play by sharing their experiences teaching it in the classroom. Sometimes they would even share the assignments they gave to students. Many of these ideas were so good that it seemed a shame not to share them. We incorporated some of the critical ideas in the *Instructor's Manual*, but many of the suggestions focused on writing assignments and exercises beyond the focus of that volume.

HOW TO USE THIS BOOK

The writing exercises in this book have been arranged to follow the general organization of *Literature: An Introduction to Fiction, Poetry, and Drama*. First, the contributions have been divided by subject into the three major literary categories—fiction, poetry, and drama. All of the writing exercises that use short fiction as their departure point, for example, appear together in one section, Second, whenever the instructor focused the exercise on a particular story, poem, or play, the exercise has been specifically linked to the selection in *Literature*.

The table of contents for *Teaching Composition with Literature* has been arranged, wherever possible, to link with specific texts in the textbook, so that instructors can more easily incorporate their exercises into their classroom plan. When a writing exercise is more general in nature (such as Sue Walker's "Dinner on the River," which potentially includes every selection, or William Rice's piece on how authors open and close short stories) the selection has been placed in a general category.

A short index, which lists authors, subjects, and titles, is also provided at the end of the volume. Many contributors discussed several selections in their exercises, especially those listed in the general sections. As its allusive title suggests, Tom Zaniello's "The Use of Force at a Clean Well-Lighted A & P" offers a provocative writing idea equally applicable to stories by Williams, Hemingway, and Updike. Likewise, in her exercise "What Will It Take to Get Your Attention?" Adrienne Bond mentions six stories that work well with her assignment. The index provides an in-depth cross-listing of these suggestions. Any instructor looking for exercises on stories, poems, or plays that are not mentioned in the table of contents should consult the index.

The exercises in *Teaching Composition with Literature* do not constitute a total course plan for instructors using *Literature* as a text in expository writing courses. (I have, however, included Kathleen De Grave's comprehensive course plan as an appendix to provide an example of how one experienced instructor organizes the writing element of her literature course.) Rather, the book is planned to supplement an instructor's class plan by providing new ideas and fresh perspectives. Every instructor finds some topics easier to teach than others. This book may prove most useful by allowing one instructor to hear another teacher's advice on approaching a particular text or topic.

HOW NOT TO USE THIS BOOK

Teaching Composition with Literature is not designed to provide critical commentary or background material to the selections in *Literature*. There is a separate and ample *Instructor's Manual* to accompany the new edition of *Literature*. If you do not have a copy of the *Instructor's Manual*, call your HarperCollins sales representative. It would be a rare teacher who did not enjoy at least perusing the manual, which provides an informal but informed commentary on every selection in *Literature*. In addition to critical ideas, scholarly notes, bibliographic summaries, and additional biographical material on authors, the *Instructor's Manual* also incorporates (with credit scrupulously given) the comments from dozens—indeed, more than one hundred—instructors who have written us about their experiences teaching the stories, poems, and plays in the book. For this wealth of practical experience alone, many will find the *Instructor's Manual* a valuable aid.

Teaching Composition with Literature is designed to supplement the *Instructor's Manual,* not to replace it, by providing practical, proven classroom ideas and assignments for instructors who use *Literature* to teach composition courses or literary courses with an emphasis on expository writing.

WHAT ABOUT CREATIVE WRITING?

As the title indicates, *Teaching Composition with Literature* is not a book intended to be used for creative writing. The editor has, in fact, regretfully turned down several excellent exercises since they focused on poetry and fiction in ways that were beyond the scope of even the most freewheeling composition courses. Many instructors, however, have mentioned that they like to incorporate one or two creative writing exercises in their course. They do so not only for variety's sake, but also because a well-designed imaginative exercise can sometimes dramatize an element of good writing or analytical thinking more memorably than a traditional composition assignment can.

I have therefore included about a half-dozen creative exercises that may initially strike some instructors as unusual. Robert Phillips, for example, offers a simple first-line exercise that can be used with either verse or prose. Although the exercise focuses on helping a student create a new poem or story, it also stresses the importance for all kinds of writing for identifying and building on a good lead. Annie Finch's sonnet-writing exercise is also a creative assignment, but the author makes a strong case that creating an original sonnet compels students to consider syntax, diction, sentence structure, and punctuation in ways they usually ignore. Several other assignments, like Fred Ding's contribution on Tennyson's "Ulysses," can be used either as creative or expository writing exercises.

There are several fine books that contain creative writing exercise. I particularly recommend *The Practice of Poetry: Writing Exercises from Poets Who Teach,* edited by Robin Behn and Chase Twichell (New York: HarperCollins, 1992) and *Writing Poems* by Robert Wallace (New York: Harper Collins, 1991).

THANKS

A great many people helped make this book possible. First and foremost are the forty-seven instructors who contributed writing and classroom exercises. The merits of the book belong to them. Some of these contributors have been long-term collaborators with *Literature*; their advice has helped the book grow and improve with each edition. At HarperCollins, Lisa Moore supported the idea of this volume, capably assisted first by Tom Maeglin and then by Lynn Huddon, while Mark Gerrard saw it through production. Katharine Glynn was the ever-resourceful development editor. X. J. Kennedy provided sage senior counsel. R. S. Gwynn, David Mason, Dianne Peich, and Bill Rice gave helpful early advice.

Dana Gioia

Literature

General Writing Exercises

What is Literature?
A Double Exercise

~~~~~~

Janis Adams Crowe
FURMAN UNIVERSITY
GREENVILLE, SOUTH CAROLINA

In my "Introduction to Literature" course, I ask students to do a short, in-class writing exercise on both the first and the day-before-last day. This exercise uses four quotations I include on an introductory information sheet:

> "Writing and reading are not all that distinct for a writer. Both exercises require being alert and ready for unaccountable beauty, for the intricateness or simple elegance of the writer's imagination, for the world that imagination evokes. Both require being mindful of the places where imagination sabotages itself, locks its own gates, pollutes its vision. Writing and reading mean being aware of the writer's notions of risk and safety, the serene achievement of, or sweaty fight for, meaning and response-ability."   *Toni Morrison*

> "Literature, in the widest sense, is just about anything written. . . . In the sense that matters to us. . . literature is a kind of art, usually written, which offers pleasure and illumination."   *X. J. Kennedy*

> "I will simply take the position that the spoken word, like the written word, amounts to a nonsensical arrangement of sounds or

letters without a consensus that assigns 'meaning.' And building from the meanings of what we hear, we order reality. Words themselves are innocuous; it is the consensus that gives them true power."

Gloria Naylor

"Literature, we're told, is one of the arts, along with painting and music; and, after you've looked up all the hard words and Classical allusions and learned what words like imagery and diction are supposed to mean, what you use in understanding it, or so you're told, is your imagination."

Northrop Frye

THE FIRST ASSIGNMENT:

X. J. Kennedy says that literature "in the widest sense, is just about anything written. . . . In the sense that matters to us. . . literature is a kind of art, usually written, which offers pleasure and illumination." Read the other definitions of literature on your intro sheet and think about your own notions of what literature is—from the college catalogue, high school or other English classes here, friends' experiences, and popular culture.

Write, in a sentence or two, your definition of what literature is—based on your reading and academic experience.

RESULTS:

Most of these first-day definitions tended to be vague and rather awkward; they relied heavily on a few words—"symbol," "great," and "creative." They mentioned few genres, usually just "novels" or "books" and "poems." Many were thought of in the contexts of academic class experience; literature has hidden meanings that classes reveal, and literature is somehow composed of works that schools own the listing of. No one mentioned literature as work that he or she might write. I read all of these in class and kept them until the end of the term when I asked them to write another definition.

THE SECOND ASSIGNMENT:

Now that we've read a great variety of writing in this class, what do you think literature is? Is it what you said it was in March? Do you have more focused ideas about what you enjoy? About what is difficult? About different genres? *Now*, how would you distinguish literature from your infirmary excuse notes, overdue book statements, letters from home, and Subway menus? Define literature this time in the context of what you have read and found of value.

RESULTS:

This time the definitions—I handed both back the last day—were more confident and more specific. Students talked about literature as if they knew some! They said it communicates feelings. It moves us. Literature "gives us a voice," one said. It "separates the human race from all other life forms." They put themselves in the definition and connected organization with particular effects. After commenting on their definitions, I tried to focus on the point that literature—as I define it—is *crafted* writing. It is writing arranged according to the vision of an individual artist. Marcel Proust says that style comes from vision, and this idea gives us a chance to talk about their point that literature lets us speak, shows us the world from each other's eyes. I raised the issue of a canonical approach to reading literature, *and* to what I think is the purpose of this intro course: the development of their analytical skills and knowledge to the point where they feel that no literature is inaccessible—even some prize-winning, experimental piece of contemporary writing. They should at least know where to get on the path into what looks at first like inhospitable territory.

Dinner On The River

~~~~~~

Sue Walker
UNIVERSITY OF SOUTH ALABAMA
MOBILE, ALABAMA

"If music be the food of love, play on."
Shakespeare

Please join us for a grande repast

Baron and Baroness D'Agneau

Place: Houseboat on the river Styx
Time: 8:00 p.m.
Dress: Optional

The occasion is a dinner party given individually by each student who may invite no fewer than eight guests. The guests may be any characters from any story or poem that has been covered during a specific period. I like to use this assignment for either a mid-term or a final exam, because it tests the student's knowledge of authors and literary works, and the students have fun determining the guest list, menu, music, and flowers and creating who says what to whom under a variety of circumstances. They can be as inventive as they like, in addition to using quoted passages from stories and poems. When I have given this assignment for a final, the students have been so enthusiastic that they asked to gather at a nearby restaurant to eat and to read their papers. The papers have been excellent and the literary party produced a post-exam party as well.

A word about placements and anachronisms. Students are free of time constraints and strictures. Any character may share the table with any other, though one may have strut and fret his hour across the stage in New Smyrna, Florida, in 1897 or in any clean, well-lighted place in 1933. Who keeps up with chronometers when Lethe water flows freely with spirits of all kinds?

I have found in giving this assignment that William Faulkner's Miss Emily is a favorite party guest in spite of the fact that she has become somewhat bitter about men and property taxes. The last time I was with her at one of these feasts, she was not in good health. Her hair was *cut short, making her look like a girl, with a vague resemblance to those angels in colored church windows—sort of tragic and serene.* She was, however, not a typical angel by any means. I sat across from her and observed her closely as she talked with an old lady who kept protesting that she did not want to go to Florida. "A Misfit's on the loose," she said, and I agreed that a woman can't be too careful these days. "You know," the grandmother went on, "a good man is hard to find." Emily said she thought she had found one once, but he wasn't the marrying kind.

Granny Weatherall was also at dinner, and, typically, she chimed in the conversation though she was sitting at least three seats down from Emily and me. Love always seems to produce such a reaction in her. Everyone says that in spite of being eighty years old, she's never gotten over that young man who jilted her. I thought the woman seemed quite demented, leaning over her plate and shouting down the table: *"I want you to find George. Find him and be sure to tell him I forgot him."* Crazy Jane was so startled that she broke off the conversation she was having with the bishop and said "Granny Weatherall, didn't anybody ever tell you that *nothing can be sole or whole that has not been rent.* You don't want to find George, and we aren't going looking for him." She went on about love being pitched in excrement. I thought it was best to change the subject, so I asked Billy to tell me about his accident in an open boat. "Who drowned?" I asked, and he said that the sea was a bucking bronco, and that he and his comrades were so busy bailing out the boat that *none of them knew the color of the sky.*

Life seems to be one tragedy after another. I can't remember her last name, but Jane told a horrifying account of the Weir Mitchell rest cures. Her husband is a doctor too, and he took her out to a run-down country estate and virtually confined her to an attic. Well, Jane pulled her chair up beside Emily and made the waiter set her a place. She said there was a woman creeping about behind some ugly yellow wallpaper and she had to peel off the monstrous paper and get her out.

I hope I wasn't rude, but the conversation got to be too much! I made my excuses as soon as we finished the chocolate mousse. It was a beautiful night on the river Styx. Charon was gallant as he reached out his hand to help me off the boat. "Great party," he said.

"Right," I told him. *Twas just brillig... and the mome raths outgrabe.* Good night."

The party assignment lends itself to any number of interesting variations. For a more in-depth discussion of a particular theme, topic, or author, I ask students to imagine that they are sitting at a table with a particular author—Kate Chopin, for example. I see Kelly over in the corner now. She wants to join them.

"Yes, Kate, I heard about the storm. Your husband was away when it happened. That must have been terribly frightening. Tell us about it."

Fiction

General Writing Exercises

Description and Characterization

~~~~~~

Adrienne Bond
MERCER UNIVERSITY
MACON, GEORGIA

This exercise can be used with "A Rose for Emily," "The Chrysanthe-mums," "Cathedral," "Greasy Lake," "Young Goodman Brown," or any story where objects, artifacts and setting are used for characterization.

There's an old game where "it" chooses the name of a person and everyone tries to guess who that person is by asking the following type of question:

> If this person were an animal, what animal would he/she be?
> If this person were a musical instrument, what kind...etc?
> If this person were a plant...
> an automobile?
> a machine?
> a book?
> an insect?
> a city?
> a house?
> a dessert?
> a color?
> a bird?

a drink?
a piece of furniture?
a tool?
a sandwich?
an academic discipline?
a garment?
a body part?
a business establishment?

. . . and so on until someone guesses who the person is.

You can use this game to improve your skills at description.

ASSIGNMENT 1.

First, pick someone you know pretty well. Then ask yourself a number of these questions and write down the answers. Now change the person's name and write a fairly lengthy description of the character (using dialogue, narration, etc., as needed). Use as many of the objects you associated with the character as possible. Have your character drive, eat, sit on, wear, use, or talk about these things. Put them in the background, or have them pass by. You may have to cut some of them out in revision, but you will be surprised how the seemingly random occurrence of these objects will improve your characterization.

ASSIGNMENT 2.

Try the same thing with a fictional character you are inventing. For good examples, look at Miss Emily Grierson (in "A Rose for Emily") or Elisa Allen (in "The Chrysanthemums").

What Will It Take to Get Your Attention?

~~~~~~

Adrienne Bond
MERCER UNIVERSITY
MACON, GEORGIA

This exercise can be used after reading "The Use of Force," "Everyday Use," "I Stand Here Ironing," "A & P," "Araby," "Barn Burning," or almost any story of self-discovery.

What will it take to convince you? What will it take to get your attention? What will it take to make you realize? Most of us find this sort of question irritating when it's directed toward us, but it is the central question the author is asking his character in a certain kind of story.

ASSIGNMENT 1:

Think back through your life. Was there an event that changed the way you looked at the world, or altered your self-image, undermined some idea or value you previously held, or caused you to act out of some higher value which had just been words to you before? What was it? Make several pages of notes abut this event and what you learned from it. Or unlearned.

ASSIGNMENT 2:

Now think hard. Can you remember (or make up) several previous times when you might have made this discovery, faced the facts, learned this hard lesson, but didn't? Other opportunities that didn't quite get your attention? Write about each of these inconclusive events in order, then end with the dramatic event you first made notes on. Voila! You have the first draft of a short story!

13

Scripting a Story

~~~~~~

Paul Buchanan
BIOLA UNIVERSITY
LA MIRADA, CALIFORNIA

I have noticed that many of my students come to college lacking confidence in their ability to write or read analytically. This trend is probably due to the fact that so much of the typical student's life has been spent in front of a television set.

But rather than belittle my students for wasting their youth, as I was inclined to do in the past, I have found that their savvy about the conventions of film and television can be exploited to discuss the elements of good writing. While they lack confidence in writing and reading, they are supremely confident in their ability to watch a movie.

I find myself creating analogies between what goes on in a typical film with what goes on in the writing process, and by discussing these analogies, I find my students more inclined to enter the dialogue. They feel that they aren't learning new techniques, but rather new ways of talking about techniques they already thoroughly know. The *establishing shot* of a new scene in a movie becomes the *topic sentence* of a new paragraph. The *visual transitions* between scenes become *thematic transitions* between topics.

I like to have my students read five or six short stories from the Kennedy reader at the beginning of the semester, posing as studio executives. After reading, we vote to buy one of these "properties" to make into a film. Once a story has been chosen, we begin scripting our film as a class. One of the students becomes the "script supervisor," whose job it is to keep the official version of the script as we go along.

The process of scripting one of these stories serves as an excellent jumping off place for talking about writing in the weeks ahead.

For example, the students are invariably concerned with making sure that the first scene is action-filled, while still introducing the main character and the conflict. Their concerns about what goes into the first scene of their movie is easily used later on to explain what should go into the first paragraph of an essay.

Students are also careful to make sure that their film is easily followed. We spend a lot of time talking about transitions between scenes, and elements that can be used to link scenes together—topics that the students naturally bring up themselves. The students are also careful to try to put scenes into a logical, causal order, and they often want to establish the order at the outset—which can become a powerful argument in favor of outlining later in the semester (a habit to which most of my students have an aversion).

Specific stories also present their own unique problems that can be used in discussions later on. For example, one class chose "The Tell-Tale Heart" and had trouble coming up with a way to present the final scene. Should the heart-beat be audible to the audience? How can the sound be suggested without implying that it was an actual sound? The obvious problem is that the story is a first person narrative, while film is almost always third person. This became an excellent way to discuss the advantages and disadvantages of the different points of view.

If I spend the first week of class talking about film, I find that my students are much less intimidated by the writing process, and I find almost every aspect of writing to have a parallel in film making, so the analogy can be used throughout the semester to explain what happens in an essay and why it happens.

Using the Elements
of Short Fiction

Mary Piering Hiltbrand
UNIVERSITY OF SOUTHERN COLORADO
PUEBLO, COLORADO

English 130 at the University of Southern Colorado is a one-semester Introduction to Fiction Course. It tends to have a large enrollment because it fulfills one of the humanities requirements for all undergraduates. Because it fulfills one of the core requirements, it attracts a high number of students who are not English majors. (In my spring section, only two out of 33 students were English majors.)

This assignment is the second of two short-story writing assignments. (For the first assignment, students are required to write a critical analysis of one of a list of designated stories. For this, the second assignment, they may either write a second critical analysis, or they may choose this option.)

ASSIGNMENT DESCRIPTION:

Write a short story. For this assignment you may submit one that you have already written. In addition, please attach a one page description of how you have used at least two of the short-story elements in constructing your story: plot, setting, characterization, tone, and symbolism are all examples of the elements you might address in this one page description. For this assignment, you will be graded not on whether you have composed a sophisticated, professional story, worthy of inclusion in this text, but on the consciousness of the short story elements that you demonstrate in describing your story. Have fun!

I find this assignment valuable for a number of reasons. First, students who have struggled to write an approximately 500-word critical analysis essay have sometimes turned in 15-page short stories! Next, it demonstrates that students often are capable of the kinds of critical consciousness that more traditional and academically oriented assignments don't reveal. Moreover, the assignment allows me to treat students as serious writers with unique and individual voices. (I comment both on their observations of their story and write some of my reflections on their use of the basic elements. Not surprisingly, my comments on their stories are often at variance with theirs. For example, a young man recently wrote extensively that the dance in his story was a symbol. I commented that I really thought that the first-person point of view was the most striking aspect of his story. It revealed a narrator who seemed decidedly obsessed and unbalanced, one about whom I felt decidedly uneasy. There was a profoundly sinister sense created by him, possibly a bit reminiscent of that of the narrator in John Fowles's *The Collector*. [I have the feeling that this student may read this book this summer.] The disparity in viewpoints often allows students to see unexpected aspects of their story, however. It also reveals to them that they, like the professional writers studied, do manipulate the short story elements, and they do have an effect on their stories.) Finally, I have urged students to submit their stories to *The Hungry Eye,* USC's fledgling literary magazine. This latter provides support for my colleagues who are working to get this publication established on campus, and it provides some further positive encouragement for students.

Here is an example of one student's description of her short story. This piece was submitted by Adele Knisley, a student enrolled in my Spring 130 Introduction to Fiction course. It reflects, I think, a fairly sophisticated understanding of the short story elements and a considerable measure of engagement with her story.

Student Essay

~~~~~~

In this short story, I have tried to utilize two different elements of the short story—point of view and symbol. First, in choosing the point of view I decided on a nonparticipating narrator with limited omniscience. Initially, I thought that Jack would be too young to comprehend the meaning of some of the events to have him tell the story himself. After working on story, I also discovered it was easier to comment on the events rather than trying to express the emotions that Jack felt (although I think this might be an approach I would like to try as well).

The symbol I incorporated into the story was the deserted, old mill. This represents the emptiness and frustration of the town, which contributes to the events at the ballpark. Breathing life back into the mill is meant to show how the people need to put the past behind them and get a fresh start. Jack's symbolic gesture in the end is his way of expressing this need.

It would be impossible to write a story without utilizing the other elements as well: character, setting, plot, and so on. For this story, however, I did not concentrate much effort on these areas. In re-writing this story, I would like to focus more attention on character, Jack's in particular. He is the more rounded character of the story. Focusing more attention on developing him might add more life to the story. Also, working more on the setting of the story, the town, and the ball field might make the symbol more clear.

~~~~~~

An Exercise in Reading the Short Story: How Authors Open and Close

William Rice
HARVARD UNIVERSITY
CAMBRIDGE, MASSACHUSETTS

The question that interests us in this assignment is one that fiction writers agonize over: how to begin and how to end a short story. With a typical minimum of eight and a maximum of thirty pages, the genre of the short story puts great pressure on each word, sentence, and paragraph. Every image, detail, and idea, all imaginable parts of a short story needs to count. Wasted words can be ruinous.

Nowhere is this more true than in both the opening and the closing paragraphs. Writers say these parts of the story can be excruciatingly difficult to get right.

Consider the example of "A Rose for Emily" by William Faulkner. Read the opening paragraph. Already there is a sense of the unknown concerning "the inside of her house." The narrator engages our curiosity. What is in the house? Why has "no one save an old-man-servant" entered it for so long? These are questions of the "what happens next" type. But there are other questions—about tone, for example. Will the voice of the narrator remain wryly matter-of-fact to the end? The social sentiments expressed and the metaphors and imagery—found, for instance, in the men's "respectful affection for a fallen monument"—all help clue us into the culture and society we are about to observe.

Now read the story through to the closing paragraph. Here we learn the macabre answer to the "what happens next" question. How does Faulkner, word by word, maintain suspense in the close of the story? Why is it that one particular detail—the "long strand of iron-gray hair"—serves so well to bring us to the horrific end? Has the narrator's voice changed? If it has, how? If it hasn't, why? What does the ending tell us about the society portrayed in the story—its "monuments," its good opinion of its own past?

If you read the story again carefully, keeping the opening and closing paragraphs clearly in mind, you'll see more and more. The short story will begin to resonate within itself, and you can write about what you've discovered.

You may want to write an expansion of these initial observations about the opening and closing of "A Rose for Emily." Or you may choose another short story in *Literature* to analyze. Some stories are especially suited to this approach, but this short list is obviously not complete:

Jorge Luis Borges, "The Gospel According to Mark"
John Cheever, "The Five-Forty-Eight"
William Faulkner, "Barn Burning"
Ernest Hemingway, "A Clean Well-Lighted Place"
Charlotte Perkins Gilman, "The Yellow Wallpaper"

In an essay or exercise, consider these kinds of questions:

1. How does the first paragraph set up the main features and problems of the story? What expectations does the writer create?
2. How does the last paragraph conclude the story—in plot, theme, significant detail, tone, idea? Do the first and last paragraphs echo each other?
3. How might the author have opened and closed the short story differently? Why do you think he or she chose to fashion the beginning and the ending in this particular way? What choices were involved?

These aren't the only questions you can ask. You can expand or limit your inquiry. No mater how narrow or broad your focus, this essay does require you to speculate about the artist's craft, and to do this sensitively and persuasively, you'll need to read closely and write from the evidence of your reading. Once you see how much care authors have put into the opening and closing of their short stories, you'll be alert as well to similar challenges of starting and finishing as these occur in poems, novels, essays, and plays—and in your own writing.

Fiction and Creation:
The Art of Naming

~~~~~~

William Rice
HARVARD UNIVERSITY
CAMBRIDGE, MASSACHUSETTS

Some painters remark on how hard it is to give names to their paintings. Working as they do in a world of color, line, and shape, rather than in the realm of words, their predicament is understandable. But even the best writers, who are masters in the world of words, face immense challenges in naming. As creators of fiction, they have to give names to their stories and characters—and, at times, to dogs, cats, and horses, towns and businesses, counties and countries, creeks and rivers, even gods and religions.

Authors sometimes try various titles before settling on the one we come to know their short stories by. (This is true of novels, poems, essays, and plays, too.) Some titles seem straightforward and even inevitable, as in Charlotte Perkins Gilman's "The Yellow Wallpaper." What other title, one wonders, could that powerful story possibly bear? But many titles are not so necessary or obvious. William Faulkner might have called "A Rose for Emily" something like "This Old House." But that title wouldn't resonate.

Think about the titles of stories you've read. Choose one that puzzles you. The most interesting titles to think and write about tend to be the odd ones—those that seem initially ambiguous, mysterious, suggestive. Consider these questions:

1. Does the title describe—or not describe—the action of the story, its theme or point, its language?
2. What might be the purpose of the title—description, prediction, bafflement?

The names of the characters usually deserve attention—even when there are no names but just a procession of "I," "he," or "she." This is the case in Raymond Carver's "Cathedral," narrated by an unnamed "I." But even here the author's choice *not* to name the narrator—or the narrator's wife—is worth pondering. Consider:

1. What is the effect or purpose of anonymity? Why is this information kept from us? Does the lack of a name create mystery?
2. Do we feel closer to or more distant from the two main characters because they lack names? At what points does the author resist the opportunity to give the characters names?

More often than not, however, characters are given names. Try scrutinizing them for meaning in the stories you have read. Ask:

1. Is the meaning overt, as in Nathaniel Hawthorne's "Young *Goodman* Brown"?
2. Is the meaning suggested, as in Katherine Ann Porter's "The Jilting of Granny *Weatherall* "?
3. Is the meaning so indirect that you want to be cautious about drawing conclusions?

Make a list of names—not just of characters, but, where appropriate, of towns, roads, and so on—and ponder their relation to the themes, events, and ideas dealt with in the short story. Look up the etymologies of given female and male names, and those that are shared by the sexes, and ask if their meanings make sense in the framework of the plot. (Most hardback college dictionaries have an appendix of names.) Similarly examine last names (surnames). Do they add a dimension to the short story?

Titles and character and place-names aren't always crucial to understanding a short story, but careful attention based on close reading can prove revealing. Stories that repay study of their respective author's choices of names include those mentioned above and also a great many others. ("A Good Man Is Hard to Find," by Flannery O'Connor, is a particularly outstanding example.)

Some of what you find in your inquiry will seem speculative, not altogether "provable," but this shouldn't deter you. Offer your readers honest—if tentative—readings, based on the evidence of the fiction and your own best hunches. We cannot read the minds of authors as we can read road maps and flowcharts. Authors, as creators, work on the boundaries of the confirmable, and to appreciate the greatness of their accomplishments we must try to understand the choices they faced, including the choice not to name—or even not to title, which was the poet Emily Dickinson's choice. You can take your heightened awareness of this naming aspect of the writer's craft into your reading of other genres (poetry is a good place to start) and into your own writing—as when you create titles for the papers you write.

The Use of Force at a Clean Well-Lighted A & P

~~~~~~

Tom Zaniello
NORTHERN KENTUCKY UNIVERSITY
HIGHLAND HEIGHTS, KENTUCKY

Whenever I feel I've taught the same story too many times the same way, I like to offer the writing assignment in which a student takes a secondary character from a short story and retells the "story" from that character's point of view. Retelling of course means confronting the original telling: What was the original point of view? Why is one character of primary importance and the student's character not? How does re-telling re-make the story? What follows is a composite version of a number of these teaching moments.

In theory any story would lend itself to this exercise, but some are more equal than others: switching Sammy's first-person narration to one of the "three girls in nothing but bathing suits" in John Updike's "A & P," for example, rearranges the furniture of the store quite a bit. Changing Angelina, William Carlos Williams's patient in "The Use of Force," into the teller rather than the told makes even the original version quite different on subsequent readings. A few brave students take on Ernest Hemingway, but find that the virtually invisible narrative style of a story such as "A Clean Well-Lighted Place" is tough to challenge. When there is consensus that Katherine Anne Porter's "The Jilting of Granny Weatherall" had better be left totally alone, I feel that at least some of the students are reading from the inside out and well.

This assignment lies in a curious zone somewhere between passive deconstruction and active reader-response. I like to treat the new stories primarily as performance pieces with classroom readings whenever possible. (I don't require the new story to be as long as the original.)

Sometimes I group the students by story title, and let them first have an internal story-slam which culminates in one group entry for the out-loud portion of the day's program.

But whether in groups or out-loud or both, we inevitably face The Big Question: Is this fair to the Author? Or a corollary: Doesn't this re-telling reflect the new teller's attitude rather than the original author's? Here I sometimes push the analytical portion of the program a bit, suggesting two characters as locked in struggle or tension, with the author clearly favoring one but not surrendering the hope of the other making a play for the reader's attention.

At different moments of the debate I launch samples of the way "reader response" has already generated the interest—and amusement—of professional writers. (Part of my hidden hand is to demonstrate that some of our professional betters have been doing this all along.) Here's a short list, with a brief comment or two, of some of the pieces I have used (and a few I haven't got around to using yet):

1. Shirley Jackson, "A Biography of a Story": These letters to Jackson c/o *The New Yorker* where "The Lottery" first appeared must be read to be believed. Having the story in *Literature* helps, but at this point virtually all of the students have already read it.
2. Mary McCarthy, *Memoirs of a Catholic Girlhood:* I suspect that most of these are fiction in the first place, but any given interchapter is her reader-response (and re-arranging) of the previous chapter.
3. Mary McCarthy, " 'General MacBeth': She Who Must Be Obeyed": She has always been a reader-response critic, often of her own work (see No. 2), but her she calls MacBeth a "golfer . . . on the Scottish fairways" and "one you could transpose into contemporary battle dress or a sport shirt and slacks."
4. James Thurber, "The Macbeth Murder Mystery": If you want more MacBeth. . . excerpts from this classic reader-response comedy can be read aloud.

5. Laura Bohannon, "Shakespeare in the Bush": A cultural anthropologist's (relativist's?) dream, as the West African elders set Bohannon straight about Hamlet's real problem.
6. Aldous Huxley, "Wordsworth in the Tropics": Not many of our students know Huxley anymore, but they certainly know some English Romantic (genteel) poetry and what Huxley is trying to do here.

A day or two of this and you will have trouble teaching point of view in the old way, whatever that way was.

Writing Assignments on Stories

The Beginnings of Self Respect:
Writing a Personal Essay
in Response to John Cheever's
"The Five-Forty-Eight"

~~~~~~

Robert McPhillips
IONA COLLEGE
NEW ROCHELLE, NEW YORK

When I teach John Cheever's short stories in my freshman writing classes, I often do so in conjunction with a number of essays by Joan Didion, including her essay "On Self-Respect." In this personal essay, Didion discusses how she herself began to develop self-respect when she failed to be elected to Phi Beta Kappa, an occasion she equates with the loss of innocence. "The day that I did not make Phi Beta Kappa," she writes:

> I lost the conviction that lights would always turn green for me, the pleasant certainty that those rather passive virtues which had won me approval as a child automatically guaranteed me not only Phi Beta Kappa keys but happiness, honor, and the love of a good man; lost a certain touching faith in the totem power of good manners, clean hair, and proven competence on the Stanford-Binet scale. To such doubtful amulets had my self-respect been pinned, and I faced myself with the nonplused apprehension of someone who has come across a vampire and has no crucifix at hand. (pp. 142-43)

Didion's experience leads her to take responsibility for her own actions, to begin to develop self-respect. In John Cheever's story "The Five-Forty-Eight," the two main characters, Blake and Miss Dent, in very different ways, are forced by their encounter, to reflect upon their actions and confront the possibility of self-respect.

Blake is, in many ways, an archetypal Cheever hero, albeit perhaps his least sympathetic one. He is a married, middle-aged white Anglo-Saxon male with a respectable job in Manhattan to which he commutes each day from the Cheeverian suburb of Shady Hill, a mythologically real Westchester town along the Hudson River with its own Metro-North train station located parallel to the river. Blake, like so many of Cheever's heros, is also strongly libidinous. In addition, like Neddy Merrill in "The Swimmer" and Cash Bentley in "O Youth and Beauty!," two other fine Cheever stories, Blake tends to ignore how his actions affect both himself and the people with whom he is involved. Despite his age and apparent respectability, he resembles the nineteen-year-old Didion in "On Self-Respect;" both of them feel "curiously exempt from the cause-effect relationships which hampered others" (Didion, p. 142). His seemingly casual affair with Miss Dent, an office temp—"a dark woman, in her early twenties, perhaps—who was slender and shy" as well as "competent, punctual, and a good typist"—and its *Fatal Attraction*-like aftermath, jolts him out of complacency, leaving himself to contemplate the fragile stability upon which his suburban paradise is built in the shabby landscape abutting the Shady Hill train station.

By contrast, Miss Dent is a character who seems to have wandered into Cheever country from the more violent, contemporary, psychic fictional terrain of Joyce Carol Oates. For during his perfunctory sexual encounter with Miss Dent, Blake learns that she has been hospitalized for emotional problems, and he deals with this knowledge in as impersonal a way as his position within the business world allows him: "When she was out to lunch, he called personnel and asked them to fire her." But she is not as easy to shake as all that. She begins to stalk him at his office, but he refuses to speak to her. So Miss Dent takes more desperate measures: she follows Blake to Grand Central Terminal and on to his commuter train, "the local—the five-forty-eight."

Miss Dent's presence on the train is eerie, uncanny: she transforms Blake's ordinary routine into an extraordinary nightmare. Her presence—she has a gun in her purse, he is to learn—forces him to reflect on his strained relationships with his neighbors on the train, and by extension, with the pathetic state of his marriage. For her part, Miss Dent, who forces Blake down on his hands in the wasteland beside the suburban train station, causing him to fall "forward in the filth" and to weep, regains a sense of psychic wholeness. " 'Now,' " she declares, " 'I can wipe my hands of all this, because you see there is some kindness, some saneness in me that I can find and use. I can wash my hands.' " She has regained her self-respect both by humiliating Blake and by proving herself capable of both "kindness" and "saneness" by sparing Blake's life and calmly walking back across to the other side of the train tracks to return to the city and to her life, free of Blake.

Miss Dent has attained a kind of psychic stability, then by the end of the story, regained a sense of self-respect. Blake, contrarily, while "saved," is also at the beginning of the journey toward self-respect.

In my usual assignment to composition students, I ask them to examine the role of self-respect in their own lives. Have they ever found themselves forced by life to reflect upon the values which determine their actions? Has any painful personal experience proven to be ultimately useful in helping them to develop a more mature understanding of life and affected their behavior accordingly? Who do they identify with more strongly in the story and why? Is Miss Dent's behavior both understandable and justified, given the circumstance of the story? Or is the threat of violence always an unacceptable option in a civilized world? Is Blake to be admired, pitied, or despised—or some combination of all three? A more advanced student may want to explore how the situation, dramatized in the story, reflects the values of mid-century America, and whether the problems it confronts are still prevalent today. (And given the high profile that has been given to the incidence of sexual harassment in the work place, one would have to say that, to a large extent, they are.) Some students might, then, use this story as a springboard for an essay on sexual-power politics in the workplace, or focus more personally on experiences of this nature that they may have encountered either in their part-time or summer jobs or in the classroom.

Depending on the assignment, then, the writing teacher can either use "The Five-Forty-Eight" as the basis for a personal narrative or a more objectively analytical essay in place of more traditional essays of literary analysis.

WORK CITED

Didion, Joan. "On Self-Respect." *Slouching Towards Bethlehem*. New York: Noonday, 1990: 142–48.

Kate Chopin's "The Storm"

~~~~~~

Dianne Peich
DELAWARE COUNTY COMMUNITY COLLEGE
MEDIA, PENNSYLVANIA

The first impulse of most composition instructors teaching Kate Chopin's "The Storm" is probably to ask students, "What do you think of *this* action?" Calixta and Alcée's sexual encounter will certainly elicit reactions from students about the morality of the action, especially since no real conflict (the focal point of all narratives) exists within the story. All of the characters are so obviously happy! Where are the recriminations? Where is the betrayal? Where *is* the guilt? In light of the social, economic, and political realities for women during the era in which Kate Chopin wrote, the story becomes even more intriguing. The subject, sexual infidelity, is timeless. Even the sexual revolution has not helped to clarify opinions about infidelity.

"The Storm" is an accessible story for freshman students and offers many excellent topics for writing, but I like to have students write about the story's setting, either in brief analyses of specific aspects of the setting or in a detailed analysis for a thesis-based paper, perhaps one which answers the question "Could the action in 'The Storm' have occurred in any other setting?" or "What influence does the setting have on the action of the story?"

I often consider this story early in the semester when I want to stress the importance of basic essay writing techniques, so I prefer to have my students first write brief papers in class which analyze specific aspects of the setting. I often ask my students to write one or more paragraphs which support topic sentences that I provide. Asking students to support these statements works nicely to emphasize the importance of coherence, unity, and development in a brief format that is easy for me to review. Following are some topic sentences about the setting of "The Storm" which are easy for students who may never have written about literature before to investigate and support with both paraphrased details and quotes from the story:

CLASS AS AN ELEMENT OF SETTING:

"Alcée and Calixta are from two different social classes." If the students have enough background information about the social dictates at the turn of the century in America, I might add another clause to the topic sentence, or ask the students to add their own, which demands a reaction to, or interpretation of the topic, for example, "Alcée and Calixta are from two different social classes and as such, would have been unlikely to marry even if they had been in love."

THE NATURAL SETTING:

"The weather causes important elements in the action." One might add, "without the storm, the tone of the story would change dramatically." Another topic sentence concerning the natural setting of the story might read, "Elements other than the weather serve to isolate the characters." One might add, "this isolation helps assure that sexual infidelity does not have to equal betrayal."

PATHETIC FALLACY:

"The storm mirrors the spontaneous emotions of Alcée and Calixta," followed perhaps by, "and serves to strengthen the intensely passionate nature of their encounter."

These topic sentences require that students analyze an entire story for a specific element (in this case, setting), isolate details relevant to that element, and effectively paraphrase and quote details supporting the topic sentence. I have found that these types of practice paragraphs encourage many of the skills necessary to write full-length college essays about literature without overwhelming the student. The instructor can give valuable feedback about such writing before the student attempts to write something longer.

Many instructors might want students to incorporate some or all of the paragraphs into a thesis-based, college-length essay about "The Storm." Students can express their own interpretation of the importance of the setting in a thesis and choose supporting details accordingly.

Writing Suggestions for "The Storm"

~~~~~~

Betty Jo Peters
MOREHEAD STATE UNIVERSITY
MOREHEAD, KENTUCKY

Sometimes our personal beliefs make teaching specific works difficult. I have always faced this problem with Kate Chopin's "The Storm." Because I had been almost embarrassed to teach this story of an overt act of adultery, I decided to focus my writing assignments about it on several other aspects. Some approaches I have used include:

- The author's failed marriage to an "Aracadian" in comparison to the protagonist's loneliness—students have to research Chopin's life and to read carefully the dialogue of the story and write their findings.
- The feminist approach—students write about the earlier feminist movement and the author's bent in that direction.
- A social statement on morality—students write a "debate," playing the devil's advocate on the right and wrong of the character's actions; they write a persuasive paper.
- The five steps to the plot as outlined in the five "chapters" of the story—students study and analyze the parts according to E.M. Forster's *Aspects of the Novel* and write a process essay.
- Also, the story as seen as a "drama" with the five "acts"—students write stage directions, blank verse and/or rhymed couplets, and dramatic lyrics for the "story."
- Akin to this, the "unities" of Aristotle—students write about the singularity of time, setting, and unity of action.

- A VHS film "Don't Drop the Potato"—Students watch this sixty-minute tape about the history of the "Cajun" people, from the time they left Europe until their settlement in southern Louisiana, and about their culture here and now, and write their reactions in contrast to mainstream America. We even bring in Justin Wilson's cookbooks, look at the pictures in the books, and even try a simple recipe or two.
- One of the most rewarding comparisons to use with "The Storm" is the Old Testament's "Song of Solomon"—Students read passages from this book and write how they believe the syntax and diction of "Solomon" influenced the writer of "The Storm."
- It can also be interesting to focus on the natural occurrence of a storm in the world of weather. My scientific-minded students enjoy writing about how a storm comes about, especially a summer storm, while also writing about symbolism and allegory.

"A Rose for Emily" and "Barn Burning"

Deborah Ford
CARROLL COLLEGE
HELENA, MONTANA

What has been most effective in my classrooms is the pairing of texts. I have used two of Faulkner's stories, "A Rose for Emily" and "Barn Burning," in this way:

After reading both stories, I have students imagine that Sarty ("Barn Burning") meets Miss Emily ("A Rose for Emily"). I ask students to write a conversation that Sarty and Miss Emily might have.

After a discussion of Faulkner's tone and style in each story, I ask students to invent a dance called "The Faulkner." I ask them to describe the dance (modern, ballet, hip-hop, and so on), to describe the costumes, the music, the scenery, the dancers. They should also describe the mood of the dance and should articulate how and why the dance has been so named.

A Writing Assignment from *Literature*
Franz Kafka's *The Metamorphosis*

Alan Jacobs
WHEATON COLLEGE
WHEATON, ILLINOIS

One of the best-known traits of Kafka's stories is their tendency to invite allegorical interpretations. One of the best-known traits of the critics who have written *about* Kafka's stories is their inability to resist such an invitation. Northrop Frye wrote many years ago that many critics dislike allegory because allegory comes with its own commentary, and thereby constricts the interpretive activities of later commentators. But the allegories in Kafka's stories, if they are there at all, are so vague and wispy as to offer no restrictions. One feels encouraged to allegorize but given few clues about how to do so. And since piecing together an allegory is one of the more pleasurable critical activities, not unlike piecing together a jigsaw puzzle, Kafka's stories have understandably become a critic's playground. *The Metamorphosis* offers innumerable possibilities for this kind of interpretive play. It doesn't take long for people to agree that Gregor Samsa is, to use the favored word, "alienated." But alienated from what and by what? From his father by an Oedipus complex? From bourgeois economic values by a recognition of the moral bankruptcy of capitalism? From bourgeois cultural values by an intellectual or aesthetic awakening? From Christian Europe by an inescapable and unassimilable Jewish identity? ("State the alternative preferred with reasons for your choice.")

This piecing-together activity is something students like to do too, in part because they have been encouraged by high school teachers to hunt for symbols, but in greater part because it is fun. And if professional critics tend not to see the dangers in such an activity, how can students be expected to do so? So what I like to do is give the allegorizing tendency free reign. Before telling my students about any of the standard allegorical interpretations listed above, I ask them to write their own allegorical interpretation of *The Metamorphosis*. The two desiderata for this assignment are, first, that their allegory account for as many details of the narrative as possible, and second, that it be inconsistent with no details of the narrative.

When we go over these allegories in class, it is always surprising and often disconcerting to the students to learn just how many interpretations account more-or-less equally well for the story's features. It is also interesting to see how often they doubt that the standard "professional" allegories of the story are any better supported than their own! This discussion often leads into some ruminations on whether Kafka intended to allow for so many different readings; why he might do such a thing, if indeed he so intended; whether we would have a lower, or perhaps a higher, opinion of the story if we discovered a letter which showed that he had had a very specific allegorical meaning in mind which no one had ever discovered (which is another way of asking how closely we link an author's inferred intentions with our evaluation of a work's literary quality); how we might interpret the story if it is *not* allegorical at all; and so on. Generally, we have a very good time.

Joyce Carol Oates's "Where Are You Going, Where Have you Been?" Three Approaches to Enrichment and Understanding

~~~~~~

Jeannette Palmer and Linda C. Rollins
MOTLOW STATE COMMUNITY COLLEGE
TULLAHOMA, TENNESSEE

The following approaches evolved from a passing conversation at the copy machine when Jeannette Palmer was making copies of Bob Dylan's lyrics to "It's All Over Now, Baby Blue" for use with her classes as they studied Joyce Carol Oates's "Where Are You Going, Where Have You Been?" Our conversation centered on trying to make literature relevant and meaningful in the lives of our students who many times complain about having to take literature courses. As we discussed Oates's story, we realized that it contains three essential elements with which we felt our students have a close affinity: everyday people (the types almost everyone knows); music, which is so very much a part of their lives; and events, such as kidnapping and rape, which surround them in their lives and are reported daily in the media. With these ideas in mind, we joined efforts, and over a semester or two of teaching and discussing the story developed these approaches.

THE ARCHETYPE APPROACH

Literature is nothing more than the study of life, a look at life's situations and how we deal with them, a look at how we handle these circumstances and how we interact with those with whom we become involved. Students—traditional and non-traditional as well—readily identify with the circumstances and characters who come alive in Oates's initiation story "Where Are You Going, Where Have You Been?" Whether we are involved with people in everyday life, or with people we encounter through literature, we see archetypes. Such archetypes dominate Oates's story.

Connie, the young protagonist—in one of the rare stories of initiations using a young woman—may be studied as the temptress/femme fatale archetype. She walks a thin line balancing her world at home and "anywhere that was not home." Her youth and beauty are countered by her innocence and lack of experience, completing her duality. Oates strengthens this archetype through numerous descriptions. Examples include:

- "Everything about her had two sides to it, one for home and one for anywhere that was not home: her walk that could be childlike and bobbing, or languid enough to make anyone think that she was hearing music in her head. . . ."
- ". . .Connie couldn't do a thing, her mind was all filled with trashy daydreams. . .
- "their [Connie and her girlfriend at the mall] faces pleased and expectant"
- "She [Connie] drew her shoulders up and sucked in the breath with the pure pleasure of being alive. . . ."

An innocent flirtation draws her into the beginning of the initiation into life when she encounters another of Oates's archetypes, the shadow (*Doppelgänger*) Arnold Friend, who, like Connie, has a dual nature. Connie sees him as ". . .a boy with shaggy black hair, in a convertible jalopy painted gold." This seemingly serendipitous meeting is what Connie perceives as yet one more playful conquest, the game she so likes to play. Unfortunately, her innocence blinds her to his ominous remark: " 'Gonna get you, baby,'. . ." This remark begins for Connie, as well as the reader, the unfolding of Arnold's darker side. On that terrifying Sunday when Arnold comes to take her for the final ride into the sunshine, "she could see then that he wasn't a kid—he was much older—thirty, maybe more." Connie realizes that there is no turning back: " 'Didn't you see me put my sign in the air when you walked by?' "

Among Oates's other references to Arnold's duality are:

- "His whole face was a mask, she thought wildly, . . ."
- "Arnold said, in a gentle-loud voice that was like a stage voice, 'The place where you came from ain't there any more, and where you had in mind to go is cancelled out.' "

Other archetypes in the story include the spinster sister, the detached father, and the resentful but knowing mother. All of these archetypes make rich sources for character analyses because to students they are real people.

THE MUSIC APPROACH

A second approach to Oates's story is the use of her numerous references to music. From its opening when Oates dedicates the story to Bob Dylan, a musical prophet of the sixties, music permeates the world of the characters just as it permeates the world of contemporary students. The following are samples:

- ". . .the music was always in the background like music at a church service, it was something to depend upon."
- ". . .but an idea, a feeling, mixed up with the urgent insistent pounding of the music and humid night air of July."
- "Connie sat with her eyes closed in the sun. . . how sweet it always was, not the way someone like June would suppose but sweet, gentle, the way it was in movies and promised in song. . ."
- "Connie. . .in a glow of slow-pulsed joy that seemed to rise mysteriously out of the music itself and lay languidly about the airless little room, breathed in and breathed out with each gentle rise and fall of her chest."
- "Connie. . .listening to the music from her radio and the boy's blend together. She stared at Arnold Friend."

- "She recognized all this and also the singsong way he talked, slightly mocking, kidding, but serious and a little melancholy, and she recognized the way he tapped one fist against the other in homage to the perpetual music behind him."
- "Part of those words [Arnold's words] were spoken with a slight rhythmic lilt, and Connie somehow recognized them—the echo of a song from last year, about a girl rushing into her boy friend's arms and coming home again—"
- "His words were not angry but only part of an incantation. The incantation was kindly."
- " 'My sweet little blue-eyed girl,' he said in a half-sung sigh that had nothing to do with her brown eyes. . . ."

The above quote is a direct reference to Bob Dylan's "It's All Over Now Baby Blue" which Oates has stated was an inspiration for her story. Students naturally want to know more about the cryptic reference. After listening to the song and being given a copy of the lyrics, students then do their own analysis of it and its relationship to the story. They may write a detailed comparison of the song and the story or take the many musical references from the story and weave them into a study of music's importance to the atmosphere or characterization. This assignment is also effective when given to a group which can produce a report to be presented to the entire class.

THE MEDIA APPROACH

Another facet of the story is its astonishingly close tie to a real-life event. (The inspiration for using this class exercise comes from Tom Quirk's article, "A Source for 'Where Are You Going, Where Have You Been?'" in the Fall 1981 *Studies in Short Fiction*.) After reading and analyzing the story, students are given a copy of a March 4, 1966 *Life* magazine article, "The Pied Piper of Tucson," by Don Moser, which recounts the terrifying reality of serial murderer Charles "Smitty" Schmid, who targeted blue-eyed, blonde teenage girls. (Quirk asserts in his article that Oates read the *Life* article as well as other accounts in the news magazines.) Students analyze the article for allusions and direct references which Oates uses or adapts in her story, such as the music, Schmid's appearance, Schmid's car, and his modus operandi.

Through this activity, whether done individually or in groups, students begin to see how writers may take actual incidents from print or other media and with their artistic abilities create a piece of literature. Alternate activities can be research projects on short stories and novels which have their bases in actual events. Stephen Crane's "The Open Boat" is a good companion piece. It is a fictionalized version of Crane's own lifeboat experience during the Spanish-American War. Also, other novels which are possible sources include: John Steinbeck's *Grapes of Wrath*, based on Steinbeck's reporting during the Great Depression; Truman Capote's *In Cold Blood*, based on a Kansas mass murder by two murderers, which Capote contended was the new novel of the future based on "creative reporting"; Oates's novel *Dark Waters*, which closely parallels the Chappaquiddick Island episode of Senator Edward Kennedy's life; the John Berendt novel *Midnight in the Garden of Good and Evil* which, by Berendt's own description, is a thinly disguised version of a sensationalized Savannah, Georgia murder; or Thomas Keneally's *Schindler's List*, based on the life of Oskar Schindler and the events of the Holocaust. Another opportunity for writing may involve students choosing a current news story from a local, regional, or national source, from which they write their own short stories based on the ideas which they glean from the source.

We carefully sequence our approach to the story by reading and analyzing *before* introducing any of the three approaches so as to let students become aware of their own insightfulness. After several semesters using these approaches, we have received continuous positive feedback from our students. They, like Connie, discover that literature is more than superficial appearance and, as readers, experience a kind of initiation themselves as they uncover the multiple levels of meaning at which a narrative may be read and appreciated.

REFERENCE

Dylan, Bob, "It's All Over Now, Baby Blue." *Bob Dylan's Greatest Hits*, Vol. II Columbia Records/CBS.

Fiction

Moser, Don. "The Pied Piper of Tucson." *Life*, 4 March 1966: 18-24+.
Quirk, Tom, "A Source for 'Where Are You Going, Where Have You Been?' "
    Studies in Short Fiction 18 (Fall 1981): 413-19.

The Faith of Fiction:
Symbolism in Flannery O'Connor's
"A Good Man Is Hard to Find"

~~~~~~

Alan Davis
MOORHEAD STATE UNIVERSITY
MOORHEAD, MINNESOTA

Flannery O'Connor is a writer whose luminous ironic vision was lost to us when she died in 1964 at age thirty-nine. Fortunately, she came of age as an artist in her twenties and "A Good Man Is Hard to Find" is one among a number of her stories which is a small masterpiece. ("Good Country People," "The Artificial Nigger," " The Displaced Person," and "Everything That Rises Must Converge" are other obvious choices.) Dramatically, this story about a petty, prideful grandmother who unintentionally leads her vacationing family into the path of The Misfit, a homicidal maniac who blames his meanness on Jesus, encapsulizes O'Connor's dark Old Testament vision of humankind.

O'Connor is about as far from New Age optimism or secular humanism as it is possible to get without falling off the edge of the earth. As such, she may be particularly appealing to members of the so-called Generation X or to other young adults who are sick to death of moral relativity on the one hand and media flatulence on the other. The Misfit, who believes that Jesus, by raising the dead, had "thrown everything off balance" so that there's "No pleasure but meanness," ends up shooting the whole family, the grandmother last, but not before she reaches out to him and murmurs, "Why you're one of my babies. You're one of my own children!" Such salvation, where the grandmother reaches past her pride to claim kinship with her murderer, is possible for O'Connor's countrified, uneducated Southerners only when extremity forces them to face mortality, the intimation of which contains, paradoxically, the possibility of redemption; with an unerring ear, O'Connor gives life to a landscape and a psychology where people are tested for the seven deadly sins, especially the sin of pride, found to be full to bursting with one or another of those sins, and given a chance to save their souls while they lose everything else, including (possibly) their lives.

Along the way, readers are in for a good deal of fun from a writer who began her creative life as a cartoonist and who never lost touch with the cadences of Southern speech, the idiosyncracies of Southern life, and the moral code of the Old South—and amalgam of the Ten Commandments, *noblesse oblige*, and fundamentalist brimstone which was practiced more in the breach than otherwise. O'Connor's South, as she feared, has become as brand-spanking generic as anywhere else, but her best fictions, which incorporate grotesque violence, racial tension, and religious hypocrisy, are as contemporary as yesterday's headlines. Any reader can open almost any newspaper and find some present-day equivalent of O'Connor's Misfit to consider. Journalists, however, seldom write about grace or redemption. They merely take editorial pleasure in the strange materialistic music of our age, whereas O'Connor's aesthetic integrity is unquestionable. "In good fiction," she has written, "certain of the details will tend to accumulate meaning from the action of the story itself, and when this happens they become symbolic in the way they work."

I want to describe a teaching approach to "A Good Man Is Hard to Find" which begins with small-group readings of the story, readings structured by an O'Connor quotation and by your chosen emphasis, and which ends with each student writing an essay that is both a critical response to group discussion and an appraisal of O'Connor's story. This collaborative approach to reading her fiction keeps students honest and demonstrates that a symbol must be earned by writer and reader alike before it can be claimed. Otherwise, O'Connor's stories, which by today's standards are too well-made, almost slick, create a steel-trap dazzle which ensnares readers into finding symbols like Easter eggs under the shrubbery of every image. Readers can emerge from her stories a little light-headed and lost, sorely tempted to reach for the nearest symbol. My teaching approach has a chance to show students that a symbol, in fiction at least, is an incarnation achieved through technique and not some sleight of hand whereby a writer injects meaning into a story with an image whose cultural symbolism is external to the fictional situation.

Introducing O'Connor, you might let anyone unfamiliar with her work know that she was a devout Catholic and a dyed-in-the-wool Southerner who believed passionately that universal truth could only be rendered in concrete detail, one image following another. Cultural symbols, if they are used, must have fictional context. We cannot assume that our readers, especially inexperienced readers without literary training, will bring any social or cultural context at all to a given fiction. In "The Fiction Writer and His Country," published in *Mystery and Manners,* O'Connor's essential book of occasional essays and lectures published posthumously, she writes that "In the greatest fiction, the writer's moral sense coincides with his dramatic sense, and I see no way for it do this unless his moral judgment is part of the very act of seeing, and he is free to use it. I have heard it said that belief in Christian dogma is a hindrance to the writer, but I myself have found nothing further from the truth. Actually, it frees the storyteller to observe." In view of this orientation, it also useful for the reader to know that O'Connor's vision is prophetic. As she writes elsewhere in *Mystery and Manners,* "there is the prophetic sense of 'seeing through' reality and there is also the prophetic function of recalling people to known but ignored truths." It is this last sense of prophecy which suggests mystery and requires good manners, for without such manners a reader might very well project anything into a story or its imagery instead of facing what is there, a process which is parallel to the process whereby her characters must face their own lives.

After introducing O'Connor, divide your class into small groups and have each group understand that it will be responsible collectively for presenting its findings, as a sort of panel, to the rest of the class, and responsible individually for writing an essay which responds to the story and to other critical opinions offered in the classroom. Provide each group with an O'Connor quotation, either from the story itself or from the essays in *Mystery and Manners,* and with lead-ins. You may give each group a different quotation and a different emphasis (symbol, character, plot, theme, language, cultural or social context) or have them all work along the same lines. Each group, for example, can think about the way symbols develop in fiction, and the story can be the common denominator. (It is also possible, given time constraints, to have several groups discussing several stories from the anthology, stories which the class will have all read but which only chosen groups will become "expert" on.) In either case, this structured approach, in my experience, keeps inexperienced readers from descending into a mere litany of likes and dislikes, or into a patchwork display of their ignorance, which serves neither O'Connor nor their own sense of literature.

Once the group has had one day to discuss the story and a second day to organize its presentation, it then presents its findings on the third day of the week and responds as well to the insights put forward by other groups. (I am assuming a class which meets three times per week, but this scheme is easily adapted to other configurations.) The papers are written over the weekend and turned in the following week, perhaps after a discussion of rough drafts. (During this discussion and drafting process, you wander from group to group, offering mini-lectures if appropriate but more likely monitoring discussion and kick-starting them as necessary, as well as offering ideas for the panel and for the essays.)

When I teach the story in this fashion, I like to use the following O'Connor quotation (again from *Mystery and Manners*) in combination with quotes from the story: "I suppose the reasons for the use of so much violence in modern fiction will differ with each writer who uses it, but in my own stories I have found that violence is strangely capable of returning my characters to reality and preparing them to accept their moment of grace. Their heads are so hard that almost nothing else will do the work." Inexperienced readers are always shocked at how quickly and (many readers think) how callously O'Connor disposes of the grandmother and her family, despite the fact that the story's first paragraph foreshadows its climax. The story is so well-made, in fact, so full of technique and craft in the service of vision and theme, that it sometimes seems to me to be the perfect "teaching" story; the quotation gives students a fulcrum whereby they can open the story, follow its lines of spiritual motion, and trace the concrete details that develop those invisible lines.

The "lead-ins" you provide can direct students to such imagery and detail, to symbolism as a process and an accumulation instead of a definition or a color-by-number procedure. Here are some examples of lead-ins which have worked for me: 1) "Is the Misfit a 'failed prophet,' someone who has seen through the reality of existence but in an unrealistic or delusional way? Analyze his conversation with the grandmother. He may be crazy, but don't just dismiss his statements as nonsense"; 2) "Does the grandmother change at the end? Is it necessary to have her killed? Is she so set in her ways that nothing else will bring her to her senses?"; 3) "Is the violence gratuitous or necessary to the story?"; 4) "A spokesperson is someone who represents the author's views. Is any character a spokesperson for O'Connor? If not, how does the story itself speak for her? Or does it?"

You can certainly find alternatives of your own which will guide your students without controlling their responses or forcing a particular reading or ideology upon them. "A Good Man Is Hard to Find" is profoundly disturbing to many students, as it should be, and allowing them to have their say without allowing them to get away with saying anything makes them think and lets the faith of fiction seep into their bones. O'Connor herself, in *Mystery and Manners*, expresses surprise at the different sorts of readings the story has received over the years. The story, however, no longer belongs to her, even though she wrote it, because it is not a tract but a fully-dramatized fiction, open to interpretation, ambiguity, and dissonance. Still, a symbol is a road map, and it points in the best fiction to real toads in our imaginary gardens; all of us, students and instructors alike, are engaged in learning to be, as the poet Marianne Moore put it, "literalists of the imagination." I am constantly surprised and enlightened by the insights that students who discipline their imaginations come to. Further, I find that the discussions, the panel presentations, and the subsequent essays benefit from a process which replicates the process we use ourselves as we read, discuss, and write about literature.

"The Use of Force" and "I Stand Here Ironing" as Models for Writing Scene and Summary

~~~~~~

Lin Enger
MOORHEAD STATE UNIVERSITY
MOORHEAD, MINNESOTA

Many of my introductory composition and creative writing students seem to share a common weakness: the relentless commitment to quick generalization and facile summaries, to easy reliance on any strategy that saves them from having to summon the particular, personal, and distinctive observations necessary to make their work interesting and authentic. Early in every term, I find myself writing the same comments repeatedly in the margins of their papers and stories.

"More..."

"Examples needed..."

"Be specific, not generic."

"What *exactly* do you mean here?"

Whether from timidity, or from lack of interest, confidence, or instruction, the essay writer in a piece about her confusing relationship with grandparents settles for this hasty accounting of her grandpa: "He is a typical old man who sits and tell stories." But where, I want to know, does he prefer to sit and what sort of stories does he tell? Do people listen to him? Has he lived an interesting life? What about his manner of speech?

Or, take the beginning fiction writer who tacks to the end of his skeletal story a complex explanation of the main character's epiphany. The writer has not taken the time to work though a sequence of fully rendered scenes; and yet he wonders why the story does not carry the emotional weight he intends for it to carry.

Student writers need to learn that the best writing is effective because it bears a strong resemblance to lived life; it rides along on a raft of authentic detail and observation. But effective writing also provides the context within which it can be interpreted and understood. It is not merely a series of details; it is a meaningful series of details. It is both the lumber and the blueprint.

To make this point, I find it helpful to lead students through a two-part writing exercise carried out in parallel to a discussion of two stories representing distinct narrative strategies: scene and summary (or exposition). "The Use of Force" by William Carlos Williams and "I Stand Here Ironing" by Tillie Olsen are an apt pair for this exercise. In both, we witness struggling working-class families. In both, young female characters suffer at the hands of harsh, disinterested forces. In both, adults must confront their own shame at how they've treated these girls. But of course the stories are starkly different from one another. "The Use of Force" is conveyed in a single swift scene, requiring little exposition. In real time the story covers perhaps ten minutes. "I Stand Here Ironing," far more leisurely in pace, is a first-person interior monologue. The narrator, as she irons a dress, reflects on her teenage daughter's life from birth to the present. The six-page story covers nineteen years in real time.

When my students arrive in class (having read the stories overnight), I immediately get them started on the first part of the writing exercises. Without making reference to either story, I ask the students to isolate in their memories a single episode in which their response to a situation was sudden anger, sharp fear, humiliation, or even violence. Their task is to describe not the events leading up to the incident, not their interpretation of it as informed by distance and perspective—but simply the moment itself, the immediate physical and emotional experience. They need to get back there in their memories and, using sensory language, describe what they see and hear and feel in such a way that a reader too will see and hear and feel the same things. A very big job, but that's what writers do.

After fifteen minutes, I have the students stop writing and turn to the Williams story. I ask a series of questions about it. Why does the doctor get angry? How does the nature of his anger change? Why does the girl resist him so violently? Why does the doctor despise the girl's parents? In what sense has the doctor "fallen in love" with the girl? These are questions to which we can usually articulate satisfying answers; to do so, however, we must read with care, for the narrator provides little exposition or direct analysis. We may note, for instance, the narrator's comparison of the girl to a "heifer" and a "savage." We may recognize that midway through the doctor's visit he has begun to "[grind] his teeth" in the fashion of the animals to which he has compared the girl. The point is, Williams manages to create the considerable resonance he does while relying primarily on dramatic devices, on the elements of scene: dialogue, description and action.

Part two of the writing exercise (which will likely have to wait for the next class meeting) asks students to return to the incidents they described earlier. This time, though, they should avoid any concrete description of the moment itself; rather, they should explain why the experience was important, what factors and forces brought it about, how they feel and think about it in retrospect. Let's say a student has written about the time years ago when she bungled her brief trumpet solo in the middle of a concert performance. She has described the cotton-dry texture of her tongue, the rising panic in her stomach, the pressure of five hundred pairs of eyes all aimed at her, the embarrassing squeak of her instrument. She has successfully recreated her sense of fear and humiliation.

But now she must view the experience from a greater distance and with more careful reflection. She might describe what playing the trumpet meant to her, how powerful it made her feel, sitting as she had in the very center of the orchestra, carrying the melody, attacking those brilliant high notes. She might reflect on how she reacted to her public failure, how she went about renovating her ego. She might suggest in what ways that small failure later prevented her from taking certain risks or shamed her into taking others.

Having tried on this thoughtful, more expository style, students now turn to the Tillie Olsen story, whose narrator takes a long view of things, looking back at her own and her daughter's lives as they have unfolded over two decades. "I Stand Here Ironing" may lack the immediacy and sudden voltage of the Williams story, but it offers its own rewards. Olsen's method allows us to receive the extended and generous insight of an intelligent woman reflecting on universal questions: Have I done well by my children? Have I done well by the people who depend on me? Should I feel regret? This is a story that goes a long way toward answering the questions it asks. It is an emotional piece, but also cerebral. It explains, summarizes, and evaluates; it seems to understand its own significance. In contrast, "The Use of Force," because of its relative lack of exposition, asks the *reader* to create the story's meaning. Williams doesn't want to give it all away.

And that is the practical difference between the strategies of scene and exposition; a scene works by the dramatic force of suggestion, exposition by a more reflective, more thoughtfully analytic power.

Strategies for Leo Tolstoi's
The Death of Ivan Ilych

~~~~~~

Deborah Ford and Kay Satre
CARROLL COLLEGE
HELENA, MONTANA

As you read *The Death of Ivan Ilych*, pay special attention to the text in order to prepare for one of the following presentations. Students will work in groups on these different aspects of the text and collaboratively devise a presentation for the rest of the class.

1. DESCRIBE:

List the characters in the novel. Then organize the list by grouping and/or arranging the characters in some fashion that makes sense to you. This will involve contrasting and comparing the characters to judge their similarities to and differences from each other. Create some kind of visual representation of this arrangement that you can share with the class.

INTERPRET:

Be sure that you can explain your particular groupings and arrangement, and that you can articulate your sense of their thematic significance to the novel as a whole.

EVALUATE:

Are these characters effectively portrayed? Why or why not? What criteria are you using to determine whether they are "effective" or not?

2. DESCRIBE:

Trace the structure of the novel. What parts can you identify? How does the novel begin and end? Draw some sort of diagram that represents the structure of the novel.

INTERPRET:

What is the significance of the overall shape and movement of the novel? What elements of the novel appear to you peculiarly Russian or late nineteenth century? What elements seem universally applicable?

EVALUATE:

Is this an effective structure for this novel? Why or why not? What criteria are you using to determine whether it is effective or not?

3. DESCRIBE:

Identify and trace several motifs through the novel. Make certain that you can show the class key passages that deal with the motifs that you identify.

INTERPRET:

What is the significance of each motif in relation to the novel as a whole? What role does each motif play in the novel, that is, what meaning does each add?

EVALUATE:

How successfully does each motif contribute meaning to the novel? How successfully is each interwoven into the novel? What criteria are you using to determine whether the motifs work well or not?

4. INTERPRET:

Identify the central themes (concepts, issues, conflicts) that this novel dramatizes. Devise a list and make connections between the various themes—how are they related to each other? Create some kind of visual representation of the complex of themes that together create the vision of this novel.

DESCRIBE:

Identify a key scene from the text that embodies each issue or that embodies several issues simultaneously.

EVALUATE:

What is your judgement of the "vision" that the novel offers? What significant insights does it provide us as readers? What questions does the novel raise? Does the "vision" of the novel involve any distortions, from your perspective, of the "truth" of things?

What I am particularly interested in is having students make *connections* when reading a text. I especially like the *visual* representations that students produce; they tap into other strengths that are not verbal and allow students to see, in concrete terms, other ways of accessing meaning.

Critical Thinking
with "A & P"

~~~~~~

Allen Ramsey
CENTRAL MISSOURI STATE UNIVERSITY
WARRENSBURG, MISSOURI

In recent years I have incorporated critical thinking activities into my composition courses. Literature provides innumerable opportunities to take up critical thinking, but one that I especially enjoy is the analysis of humor. After my class has read "A & P," I inquire about its comic effects. My students typically find the story mildly amusing.

The question in this analysis is not, "Is it funny?" but, "If it's funny, why?" As an introduction to the discussion, I provide a hand-out which has the following newspaper article:

Man Faces Charges in Assaults on Teens

A man accused of knocking down teen-age girls, taking off their shoes and sucking their toes has been arrested.

"It's kind of a humiliating thing. I think emotionally it just degraded them," said St. Louis police Maj. Ronald Henderson. "My main concern was what was next."

Edgar Jones, 28, was charged with assault, indecent exposure and sexual abuse Wednesday in connection with the bizarre crimes, which started occurring in January and continued until two weeks ago.

The eight girls who were victims all identified Jones in a lineup, Henderson said.

"A couple of them broke down," he said.

Jones, a laborer, posed as a jogger in his early morning attacks on the girls, whose ages ranged from 13 to 19, Henderson said.

In the most recent attack, a 13-year-old girl waiting for a school bus was knocked to the ground by a man. He told her he wouldn't hurt her but wanted to suck her toes.

After the girl stopped struggling, the man took off her left shoe and sock and sucked her toes. He did not otherwise harm her, and after a brief time he released her.

In other incidents, "he would run by and touch them and then turn around and come back," Henderson said.

This short statement is provocative because it causes some students to convulse with laughter, some to titter and then clap a hand over their mouth, and some to read solemnly without any expression whatever.

I have asked students to write for 10 minutes on this article ("Is this article funny? Why?") before a discussion. The pivotal word is "bizarre," a word that summarizes why some things, at least, are funny. In this case, aberrant behavior is at once preposterous, grotesque, and, for some, offensive. As discussants sort through the curious reactions to the story, the political correctness issue normally emerges: How can you laugh at *victims*? The fact is, practical jokes are comedies of victimization. The practical joke is also a topic of discussion.

Should we laugh at this article? I have never taken a position on this question, and I have never had a class agree. Most interesting to me, though, is seeing a student start to laugh (sometimes uproariously), but then hesitate, choke down the laughter, and then write a solemn essay about those poor girls who were attacked. The question arises: Do we laugh only when it is socially acceptable to do so? Just how inhibited are we by what others think?

In turning to "A & P," we ask if and why this story is funny. Sammy's narrative voice reveals a level of immaturity with his sexuality, his job and his employer, and his co-worker Stoksie; his naivete and altruism evoke either amusement or derision (depending on the reader). The analogy to the newspaper article becomes evident: if readers can recognize Sammy's immaturity as immaturity rather than simply chauvinism (chauvinism, as in "chauvinist pig"), the comic elements may emerge. In both cases, the reader must be able to move beyond "How am I supposed to react?" to "Am I human enough to recognize human weakness as part of the human circus?"

There is a final kicker. We are right to ask whether at some point our laughter should become subdued by other emotions, such as compassion, pity, anger, or outrage.

Now that I have talked my way through this pedagogy, it seems to me that this discussion could be useful as a preface to a series of stories: "Gimpel the Fool," "A Good Man Is Hard to Find," "The Catbird Seat," and as a contrast, "Where Are You Going, Where Have You Been?" (The truly unfunny bizarre).

Sample Assignment for
Alice Walker's "Everyday Use"

~~~~~~

Allison M. Cummings
UNIVERSITY OF WISCONSIN-MADISON
MADISON, WISCONSIN

At the University of Wisconsin-Madison, most of the freshman compo-sition classes focus on writing either about adolescent change or about notions of cultural literacy. I tried to combine the two in my course, by having students write and think about how they interpret their own lives through narratives. The first assignment was to write a four-page essay about a turning point in life, or a moment when the student suddenly became conscious of himself or herself as a _____ (black, white, latino, Asian, Jewish, Catholic, female, male, lower-middle class, or any other category that seemed different from one's general social context.) I like to discuss Walker's "Everyday Use" in class before handing out the assignment because it illustrates with such deft humor how people may invent themselves. It also hits home with students (and teachers) who are caught in the midst of debates about multiculturalism: what does it mean? Is race a matter of the stories you tell yourself, or the stories your family or culture tells you, or. . . ?

In the story, the mother is pragmatic, unpretentious, but tolerant of her daughter's abrupt changes (which she sees as fairly consistent with Dee's odd personality all along). Dee, a.k.a. Wangero, newly Afrocentric, suddenly finds the details of her family's roots part of a cultural narrative about adversity and resourcefulness, from which she now derives pride. She snaps Polaroids of this house, identical to the one she perhaps sabotaged as a teen. We discuss why Maggie bears the burn scars from the house fire Dee may have lit. Although students initially react against Dee/Wangero as a phony, as we talk about her values and assumptions, it becomes clear that many students share them. We reconsider the difference of the mother's daydream of being brought on TV for a reunion with Dee, and her self-description—"who ever knew a Johnson with a quick tongue?"—that now makes her seem like a trickster narrator.

Finally, we talk about the principal opposition the story sets up—between "use" and decoration, which Dee/Wangero refers to, significantly, as "hanging" (paragraph 73). Although the mother seems tolerant of Dee/Wangero's strange values, when Dee claims the quilts that were promised to Maggie, the mother says "something hit me in the head" (paragraph 77), and she snatches the quilts away and throws them and Maggie on the bed. What hits her and why? Why does she hug Maggie, something she never does? How do the mother's and Dee/Wangero's different relations to the quilts (or to the butter churn, the benches, or the house) characterize their relations to each other, to society, and to their own lives?

If there's time left, we talk about why Walker chose to use quilts as the site of mother and daughter struggle, and how quilts encode identity. The bits of Grandma and Big Dee's clothes, plus the tiny piece from their Great Grandpa's Civil War uniform, all silently document the family's past and its role in history. The women's intergenerational work on the quilts and passed-on knowledge of how to make them signifies the self-knowledge that comes from a sense of continuity with and ability to carry forward the past. And the metaphor of quilting, as piecing together bits of clothes, themselves associated with roles and identity, has been used by many feminist writers to connote these multiple relations—of people to identity, to their pasts, to knowledge, creativity and self-expression through everyday objects of art *and* use.

The students generally begin talking about the story sure of who they like and dislike and why. But as we talk more, the story becomes more complicated, particularly if they compare the stance on identity that each character represents to their own stance—is identity derived from what you have and do, or from a story of a legacy, or what? Whether they resolve the story for themselves or not, they get thinking about *what has made them think the way they do about who they are.* Although it is often hard for students to recall a moment when "something hit them" (that realization may be far in the past), they can usually recall small reminders or brief moments when some comment or gesture reminded them: "Oh yeah, I'm female." Students tend to think of moments of differentiation as painful or self-destructive; I encourage them to also think about moments when they felt part of a group and felt good about that differentiation from the larger culture.

I also remind them of how Wangero's interpretation of her heritage seems false, and caution them against relying on abstractions. I urge them to situate their descriptions of themselves in specific images (from pictures, memory, family stories) of before and after—like Dee's relation to the house, before and after her transformation. I tell them to tell a story with two parts, and then to reflect on the difference between them. The paper should clearly contrast the two moments (and comprise about two pages), then switch gears from storytelling to interpretation.

This is the tough part: achieving balance between description and analysis. Most students will do solely one or the other in their first drafts. When they read and critique each other's papers in groups of three—which they do all semester—they see the shortcomings of having only story or only analysis. The summary has no thesis or conclusions (and here is a useful distinction between fiction and analytical papers for them), and the paper has no detailed examples, which every college paper must have. If they have only stories, they develop an analysis through drafts by taking points from the conclusion and putting them first. If they have only abstractions, it isn't hard to point out the need for specific examples. I talk about this kind of draft with the class as a whole, and compare the use of examples to the use of quotations from texts, to give them a sense of the pattern of college papers. This process teaches the students how to work from examples to a thesis and how to re-shape their stories or plot summaries into analytical papers.

I think "Everyday Use" is a deceptively simple story that has enormous potential to involve students in heated discussion of complicated issues. We make the story into useful material itself, piecing it into the student's own quiltings of their lives.

A Three-Part Approach
to Writing on Alice Walker's
"Everyday Use"

~~~~~~

Peggy Ellsberg
BARNARD COLLEGE
NEW YORK, NEW YORK

Alice Walker's "Everyday Use" is a story that I assign in two classes I teach: one called "Writing Women's Lives" and the other called "Ethnicity and Social Transformation." The story introduces themes applicable to both topics. Both of these courses are designed primarily for first year students, and my goal in formulating their written exercises is to teach the expository virtues of conciseness, clarity, and focus. I suggest that a paper on "Everyday Use" be two to three pages in length. At least once each semester we rehearse a written exercise together in class.

First, after we have read the story, I ask the students to paraphrase or summarize its plot or content. I write an outline of their statements on the board, compiling them until I reach a consensus that goes something like this: an African-American mother, living in simplicity or even poverty in rural Georgia, describes her two daughters. Dee is stylish, confident, and ambitious, has gone to college, and has left home. Maggie is timid and a homebody; soon she will marry a local guy and follow in the footsteps of her forbears as a farmwife. Dee comes back home to visit, arrayed in African garb, accompanied by a comical Black Muslim boyfriend, and the two sisters clash over the divergent values in the two black cultures that each represents.

Second, I lead my students from a superficial plot summary into a deeper look at the meaning of the story, starting with the special devices and economies of the narrative. I ask them to choose particular sentences, phrases, and words that illuminate the larger meaning of Mama's descriptions: "I am a large, big-boned woman with rough, man-working hands"; "My fat keeps me hot in zero weather"; her comparison of Maggie to a "lame animal"; her recollection of the fire that destroyed their other house and scorched and scarred Maggie. When Dee arrives she is wearing "a dress so loud it hurts my eyes." Dee has taken an African name, "Wangero Leewanika Keemanjo," discarding the matriarchal ancestral name that Mama gave her. My goal in this part of the exercise is to encourage, to require, students to search for important moments in the narrative and then to fasten every allegation they make about a piece of literature to a proof from the text. By focusing closely on precise details that illuminate the story efficiently, they learn to illustrate their own statements accurately and efficiently.

Finally, the end of the exercise is to analyze or evaluate the message of the story. Having summarized its plot and isolated examples from its special narrative technique, students are now ready to make suggestions (and support them with proof) about the broader meaning of this piece of literature. What polarities in current African-American culture do these two sisters represent? How does Mama feel about her two daughters, and how are we expected to feel about Mama's judgments? Does the author respect, or want us to respect, any of these characters more than others? Does this story make a contribution to current debates about Afrocentrism or womanism (black feminism) or about multiculturalism?

In a short explication of a short text—whether a poem, an essay, or a short story—I ask my students to employ a three-part model: 1) paraphrase or summarize; 2) discuss particular literary techniques, especially as they illuminate the meaning of the piece; 3) evaluate or analyze the message. I find that this formula helps to anchor students to an accessible procedure that combines specific observation and creative analysis.

Finding the Point of View

~~~~~~

Jim Hauser
WILLIAM PATTERSON COLLEGE
WAYNE, NEW JERSEY

I find that Alice Walker's "Everyday Use" is a terrifically rewarding story to teach, at least with the kinds of first-generation college students in my classes at a state college. "Everyday Use" may not have quite the immediate appeal of a story like T. C. Boyle's "Greasy Lake," but it both emotionally and intellectually reaches out to students.

However, while this story appeals to my students and works in the classroom, it is also a story with significant emotional and intellectual problems. But it may well be these problems which finally make "Everyday Use" most valuable for beginning college readers.

Emotionally, many of my students (like myself) are drawn in by the sibling rivalry and by the opportunity to identify with the ugly-duckling child and to participate in the apparently justifiable triumph of this neglected and victimized sister/daughter (as well as the sympathetic, beleaguered mother). In addition, for students who may themselves be caught up in the tension of entering college, and the fear of separation from family which that brings to many of them, the story strikes a powerfully retrogressive emotional chord. It also reaches them in its focus on everyday possessions and on the differing attitudes possible toward material objects and materialism.

Intellectually, too, the story seems very attractive to my students: its schematically defined oppositions are blessedly free of the thematic murkiness of much of the fiction I assign, and the story affords them a welcome and useful chance to exercise their symbol-reading skills. Few modern fictions afford so clear a study of the ambiguity of symbolic objects. The diverse and conflicting possibilities of meaning that Nathaniel Hawthorne and Herman Melville find in the scarlet letter and the whiteness of the whale, respectively, Walker finds in the quilt and the butter churn. Rarely is it as rewarding as it is here to have students hunt for symbols and define the meanings that different characters attach to them.

Throughout high school, our students have been trained, at best, to identify, and identify with, the point of view of the authors and fictions they've been assigned. If, say, they've read Ken Kesey's *One Flew Over the Cuckoo's Nest* and been offended by its anti-institutional stance, they've been told "that's not what Kesey is saying." "Everyday Use," I believe, provides a fine opportunity for us to teach a more interrogative and adversarial reading strategy: Walker's story seems to beg for what Judith Fetterley calls "the resisting reader."

In defining its opposition between traditional and changing values, this story is as sure of itself as a Rush Limbaugh radio broadcast, and yet it seductively wraps its fears, angers, and biases in a heartwarming sympathy for the neglected Maggie and for the commonsensical, humorous, attractive mother through whom Walker narrates the tale. This story presents an implicit debate about values, but it achieves its lopsided victory for tradition by drawing the character of Dee in a broadly unattractive manner. If we were teaching logic, we would surely want to discuss the nature of *ad hominem* arguments here.

In order to break through the implicit conservatism that this story so beguilingly presents, I want to challenge the students to recognize the ways in which they may be like Dee/Wangero. Their responses vary greatly and many students can, at most, recognize that situationally they resemble her a bit, for they too have left for college (though, they often protest, going to college does not mean *leaving* family or changing values). However, with the help of either the teacher or, hopefully, their more insightful or more rebellious peers, most students begin to recognize that they have a great deal of Dee within themselves. They too may wish to strike out on their own; somewhere inside them they know that protective parents may be undermining their bids for autonomy; and they may even begin to understand the healthy impulses that underlie changing.

And I believe that if we can get them to identify with Dee, even a little, we can move them toward the interrogatory position that I believe we'd like them to bring to all their reading. In this case, they often need some historical/cultural background as well. We may want to point out that it is not surprising that the mother sees willfulness and cruelty in Dee, for she wishes to maintain her traditional rural position which involves racial subservience to the whites she knows she could never look directly in the face. This may need some explaining, as may the fact that the assumption of a Muslim name may be a meaningful political action and not merely a whimsically egoistic one.

One way to drive home the point that these characters and this situation may be open to other readings than Walker's is to ask them to rewrite a section of the story from Dee's point of view. I've found that I have to insist that my assignment requires that they experiment with seeing through Dee's eyes, for Walker is very convincing here, and it's often hard for students truly to imagine Dee sympathetically.

I have the students spend a good bit time in groups working to see Dee/Wangero from perspectives other than Walker's. They discuss specific scenes, looking for what we may broadly call Walker's "biases." Though some surprisingly strong fiction may result from this project in revisioning a well-known author's writing, it is important to remember that the goal is to use fiction writing in order to train resisting readers.

One student's breakthrough occurred in rewriting sections of the story which depict Dee's attitude toward the objects of "everyday use": in this student's rewriting, Dee was shown as heroically independent—since all quilts, even historically significant ones, do wear out when used at home, Dee's aestheticism was presented as intelligent, necessary, and loving. In discussion, this student suggested that she could imagine someone like Dee someday becoming a museum curator whose goal was to save a disappearing heritage.

The crucial issue here is not that students be led to believe that Walker is in any sense "wrong." Rather, it is important that they be led to recognize that *her* point of view, *any* author's point of view, is *a point of view*, that as intelligent readers they certainly need to identify and understand, but also to explore, question, and resist.

A Useful Videotape for Both Readers and Writers

Thomas Carper
UNIVERSITY OF SOUTHERN MAINE
PORTLAND, MAINE

Like many, I try to teach writing in my literature classes and at least some literature in my freshman-level writing classes. For both I have found very useful a half-hour videotaped profile of Eudora Welty (*The Writer in America: Eudora Welty*, Coronet Film and Video, 1975). For literature classes it provides an introduction to a celebrated writer, to her opinions about the role of a woman writer (to be universal and "transcend everything you write"), and to her views about how one discovers a subject. Ms. Welty also gives moving readings from her short stories and her novel *Losing Battles*.

But much of the tape is directly relevant to writing of all kinds, as it focuses illuminatingly on how this writer observes, prepares drafts, and revises. We see her demonstrate her powers of observation as we watch her interpret some of her own early photographs; this helps students understand how any writer must look closely at small details to gain insight into what is happening with the situations or people being observed and analyzed. We hear her speak of how she can write anywhere, when traveling or away from home, but that in her own room she will shape the material, type it out, make it objective—"a physical thing"—look at it, and revise it. "It's adventurous to revise," she says, and it's fun and instructive to watch her take a typescript of several pages, lay it out on a table, cut a paragraph from one sheet and insert it into another, pin it in place—and then report that she will methodically retype the long sheets and, perhaps, revise again.

Today, when most students write their class papers at a computer, it is salutary to be reminded that cutting and pasting on the screen may not be "physical" enough, that the beautiful print-out of a first draft may be treacherously easy to produce.

Finally, among many pertinent and insightful remarks, the last one we hear should be meaningful to all who care about their writing: Ms. Welty concludes, "I always respond to my own words."

Poetry

General Writing Assignments

Symbols and Figurative Language

~~~~~~

Janis Adams Crowe
FURMAN UNIVERSITY
GREENVILLE, SOUTH CAROLINA

Have the class read the definition of symbol in the chapter "Symbol." Discuss poems that are complex and difficult ("Sailing to Byzantium" and analysis), and ones whose meanings are often partly elusive. Discuss language that points us toward conflicting ideas, toward ideas that are hard to pin down—green thoughts. Read X. J. Kennedy's all-time great discussion of figurative language extending meaning by going beyond the literal, and then read Howard Nemerov's "Snow Globe." What does the globe suggest or symbolize?

EXERCISE:

Take an object you remember from your childhood—something that you loved or found especially interesting—and describe it in conversational prose. Tell your readers what it meant to you explicitly. Then find a metaphor or simile that expresses the value you found in your object by actually using the object, as Nemerov does. What happens when you move from explicit statement to figurative suggestion? Which piece of writing needs more words? Why? Is it easier to write about the object in prose or poetry?

Sonnet-writing Exercise

Annie Finch
UNIVERSITY OF NORTHERN IOWA
CEDAR FALLS, IOWA

After one or two classes devoted to discussion of the sonnet in an Introduction to Literature course, or after some discussion of the form in a basic writing class, I ask the students to write a sonnet themselves. They are often shocked at this; few have written any poetry before, and if they have it is likely to have been in free verse. I allay any fears by telling them that the exercise is merely a way for them better to understand the structure of the form, and that their effort does not have to be profound or "poetic." Anything they write about will be fine, as long as it is fourteen lines of correctly rhymed iambic pentameter, either Petrarchan or Shakespearean.

By this time, we will have read many of the sonnets in *Literature*. My favorites are those by Michael Drayton, Robert Frost ("The Silken Tent"), Emma Lazarus, Wilfred Owen, Thomas Hardy ("Hap"), John Keats, Elizabeth Barrett Browning ("How Do I Love Thee"), John Donne, and Gwendolyn Brooks. There are also fine sonnets by Weldon Kees, William Wordsworth, Shakespeare, Thomas Carper, R. S. Gwynn, John Milton, Howard Nemerov, and others to choose from. The class has had a chance to discuss the frequency of iambic pentameter in English speech, to listen for the meter in each other's speech, and to discuss its most common metrical variations (anapests to speed things up, spondees to slow things down, trochees to catch attention). Sometimes I let the students memorize a sonnet for extra credit. After a few classes of such preparation, the students generally find writing their sonnet surprisingly easy and feel triumphant that something they feared has been demystified.

The variety of tones and approaches in the finished sonnets is remarkable. The unusual attention to form frees the students from worrying too much about the content of what they are saying, and they can produce very interesting and revealing poems through this exercise. I choose several student sonnets to pass around and discuss during the final class on the sonnet. Before class, I ask the writers if they would enjoy reading their creation aloud, and usually they are glad to do so. Our class discussion of the students' sonnets offers an excellent opportunity to discuss not only the sonnet form but also sentence structure and syntax, diction, verbal connotations, and punctuation. Since this is not a poetry-writing course, I grade the sonnets pass/fail, and I don't worry about how perfectly they scan. The effort is the main thing. I have had several students comment that writing a sonnet was one of the most satisfying exercises in the course.

Student Assignment

Here is a sonnet written for this exercise by a student who had never written one before:

> Poetry is very awful to learn,
> with the meters and meanings invisible.
> As your spirits sink with each page you turn,
> You feel as though you are an imbecile.
> The longer they get the more lost I am,
> But even the shorter ones confuse me.
> Writing poems is hard, I'd rather eat Spam
> And skip the great chance to learn poetry.
> I then met a professor, Annie Finch,
> who taught the class, Introduction to Lit.
> The guidelines were set, and it was a cinch.
> I found out poems don't even hurt a bit.
> I now know the writing poems can be fun,
> And someday I may write another one.

Sense and Unsense

~~~~~~

John Gery
UNIVERSITY OF NEW ORLEANS
NEW ORLEANS, LOUISIANA

One of the pleasures of teaching poetry, especially the close reading of poems, is that surge of gratification I feel when a student's eyes light up at the moment of understanding the seductiveness in a poem such as John Donne's "The Flea," the pathos in Ezra Pound's "The River Merchant's Wife: A Letter," or the horror in Sylvia Plath's "Lady Lazarus." To watch a student discover his or her intimate feelings of desire, pain, or anger in the language of the lyric fills me with optimism about the ability of poetry to embody and communicate our interior lives.

Often, however, I have learned that a thorough discussion of a poem in class will prompt one or two students afterwards to ask, "Did the poet *really* mean all those things we said? Aren't we just making up our own interpretations?" Or, "I never would have found what other people found in that poem. I myself couldn't make any sense of it all." I reply, of course, that while there is always room for a difference of opinion concerning a poem's sense, we can usually arrive at certain premises the poet must have had in mind, if not while composing, then by the time the poem was completed. Yet the students who ask these questions remain either skeptical about the authority of readers or afraid that they themselves will never understand how poems make meaning.

One exercise that addresses this concept of intentionality, sense and "unsense" is an assignment I have used while reading poems even less accessible than those by Donne, Pound and Plath—poems such as

76

T. S. Eliot's "The Love Song of J. Alfred Prufrock," E.E. Cummings's "anyone lived in a pretty how town," and the poems of Wallace Stevens, or the syntactically idiosyncratic poems of Emily Dickinson, Dylan Thomas, and John Ashbery. Coming to these difficult poems, I usually start by dissuading students from trying too hard to "make sense" of them. Instead, I emphasize how difficult it is, in fact, for a poet *not* to make sense, or to make "unsense."

The assignment I give is for each student to compose a ten- to twelve-line poem that, if possible, makes absolutely no sense. It is not to write "nonsense," which usually attempts to be funny and therefore has a guiding principle, but to make "unsense," that is, to assemble a series of lines that have no clearly affective qualities or intended meaning. Students may and should use imagery and normal syntax, as well as rhyme and rhythm if they want, rather than just collect words at random (that's another exercise with different goals). If they prefer, they may even write a poem that imitates the syntax of "The Emperor of Ice Cream" or "Fern Hill" exactly, for instance, but that employs wholly different images and words. The challenge is to write a poem in which no image, word, or phrase has any apparent continuity with or ostensible relation to any other, as in Gertrude Stein's line, "Dining is west," or the couplet, "In slipped plates, eels festooned the tunnel's laughter/ where tasks, I leapt to note, cringed dully after."

This assignment usually proves far more difficult than it sounds at first, yet most students enjoy trying it, since it liberates them from having to make sense, for a change. After I collect the poems, it is easy to write a few affirmative remarks about their wild effusions in the margins, and more ambitious students will inevitably come up with poems that, on a first reading, sound very much like Wallace Stevens or Dylan Thomas in their creative assemblage of unrelated sounds, images, and diction.

What I do next, with the student's permission, is to reproduce two or three of these "unsense" poems to distribute to the class. We might read them aloud. But without further discussion, I then ask students to choose one and to write a brief (one-page) "explication" of its development and theme. Here again, because students realize that the poem is "not supposed to have meaning," they are encouraged to be as creative in their interpretations as they want, just as long as their essays develop a sustained reading of the poem. In my experience, the results are often surprisingly focused. Because they do not have to worry about the "correct" reading of the poem, they often feel free to read directly from its structure and language and are therefore able to make remarkable connections. Meanwhile, those whose poems are discussed and written about are generally elated that their own inventive words have evoked such cogent and "deep" responses. After this exercise, once we return to the poems in the text, our discussions of meaning tend to take on a more relaxed tone.

The goal of this exercise when it works (and it doesn't always) is threefold: (1) to give students hands-on practice in a nonevaluative manner both in creative writing and analytical writing; (2) to allow them to interact with their peers through a text instead of through discussion alone; and (3) to enhance their awareness of the reading of poetry as part of an interpretive community, in which readers do indeed have the right and power to "make sense" of what they read, tapping both into the intentions of the writer and into the broader cultural ideas each of us brings to poetry. A further result can be that students who at first might approach poetry such as Stevens's or Ashbery's with a suspicion that they are being talked down to (by poets who seem mysteriously privy to what they themselves don't know) might feel less hesitant about offering their interpretations of difficult works, even when they are unsure of the meaning. Once they realize how unfathomable "unsense" actually is, sense itself should seem less sacred and more amenable.

"The First Line Exercise"

～～～～～～～～～～～～～～～～～～～～～～～～～～～

Robert Phillips
UNIVERSITY OF HOUSTON
HOUSTON, TEXAS

One exercise which has yielded interesting student writing is what I call "The First Line Exercise." I ask students to write on a sheet of paper the first line of any poem with which they are familiar. Then I ask them to write a new poem utilizing that as the first line.

It is difficult not have something to say after putting down "Nature's first green is gold," or "When you are old and grey and full of sleep," or "I wandered lonely as a cloud." I insist the students put the borrowed line within quotation marks, to avoid any misunderstandings (or delusions of grandeur) about who wrote what.

The idea isn't to rewrite or paraphrase the original poem. The idea is to create a totally new poem utilizing someone else's first line as a springboard. After the poem is completed, it is handed in together with a copy of the famous poem. In class both are read and analyzed, interpreted, compared, and contrasted. The student poem isn't expected to be "as good" as the other, just different. And in many ways it may be just as interesting and surprising.

The same exercise can work for short fiction as well. Think of the possibilities for taking off after putting to paper, "None of them knew the color of the sky," or "I read about it in the paper, in the subway, on my way to work," or "As Gregor Samsa awoke one morning from uneasy dreams he found himself transformed in his bed into a gigantic insect." Begin in the middle of an arresting situation, and a real story is likely to develop.

Teaching Poetic Voice

~~~~~~

Fred W. Robbins
SOUTHERN ILLINOIS UNIVERSITY
EDWARDSVILLE, ILLINOIS

I find myself fighting the temptation to compare generations of students. However, I do agree with the opinion that current students seem more resistant to and prejudiced against poetry. Some of them insist that poetry matters much less than their pop music lyrics. (Perhaps they merely want to tweak the beard of their ancient professor.) In response, I try to dramatize the voice in poems by reading aloud, hoping to give them a sense that poetry speaks to them, sings to them, much as their pop music does. The hardest part of poetry for many beginning students—and for many more advanced students—is tone of voice. Often they will ask to hear a recording of a poet reading his or her own work. That's fine and it has its place, but at an early point in the course, I don't want the students to get the idea that poetry is only an activity for their entertainment. Many of them are too passive to "get" poetry, anyway. I resist such audio-visual aids and reserve them for relatively advanced students only; students in senior-level courses should be experienced enough to listen, as well as read, critically. But for these freshmen, I dramatize the voice, reading aloud in a moderately melodramatic way.

In introducing the study of the chapter "Listening to a Voice," I will read a poem or two in such an exaggerated manner that the voice becomes a sort of caricature of sententiousness or of sarcasm. Jonson's "To Celia" works pretty well when read aloud one way, then the other—as the conventional courtly love song, then as a complaint and as an assertion of the speaker's boredom with Celia. Richard Lovelace's "To Lucasta" can almost always spark an argument about tone, about degree of irony. Trying to read James Stephens's "A Glass of Beer" without sarcasm is a test for anyone. Reading William Wordsworth's "I Wandered Lonely as a Cloud" with sarcasm is, for me, impossible, yet in straining to do so, I sometimes give the students the sense of voice that must be the foundation for a complete and responsible reading. It probably matters little whether I read aloud well or not, but it does matter that I show the students how one tries to get this sense of voice, working with the extremes of tone—solemnity and sarcasm. I am willing to seem foolish in order to get that across to them.

I always begin the course with poetry, as I am used to introducing the students to critical terminology through the study of verse. The first paper assigned in the semester will be about voice and tone. By the time the paper is due, we will normally have progressed to studying diction and imagery, so the students often make the obvious connections between tone and levels of diction; of course, that is one of the aims of the writing assignment, although not an explicit aim. They are assigned a paper of 500-600 words on a poem in the text; the paper is to be in three parts. Part one interprets the poem straightforwardly and seriously (the "solemn" reading); part two interprets the poem as sarcasm; part three, the meat of the paper, argues for one reading or the other, basing the argument on the diction and figurative language as well as on the sense of voice, the character, the persona in the poem. Often, the students will conclude their papers by admitting that their poems are not wholly solemn or wholly sarcastic, but are a mixture of tones, and they will begin to see how subtle and ephemeral this business of poetic tone can be. If students really demonstrate an understanding of that fact, their papers seem to me to be sound criticism. If the students go on to point out that the language of real people in real situations is often a complex admixture of levels and tones—lovers, men going to war, drunks with grim thirsts, someone struggling to describe an amazing sight such as a locomotive—then they are excellent students and have some talent for language. Most students, the "C" students, will not make these connections, but will just struggle to throw together in a paper some adjectives that describe tone.

If I were to teach this lesson and make this assignment in a literature/composition course, I would certainly help them to plan to mix the comparison structure with the argumentative structure. I would explain the nature of evidence, and talk about the fact that mere assertion does not convince or persuade or offer much insight. A mimeographed handout with a list of the descriptive adjectives commonly applied to tone (such as "joyful," "expectant," "angry") and their synonyms and antonyms is worth a quick tour through a thesaurus. It might keep some students from turning the paper into a struggle and a chore in their minds. Another aid is commenting on the text's discussion of irony, which focuses on the idea of point of view in poetry and makes useful distinctions among several kinds of irony. Another lesson that is worth a few minutes is based on the section "How to Quote a Poem" in the "Writing about Literature" chapter. Most students are completely ignorant about that convention, and such ignorance will inhibit their thinking and keep them from taking care with the more central aspects of composition.

When I began to teach this course in the seventies, I relied on the obvious expedient of studying a dramatic monologue to reveal the complexities of irony and the manifold possibilities of tonality in verse. Now, such a poem as Robert Browning's "Soliloquy of the Spanish Cloister" seems too complex to begin the course. I reserve such poems with their "unreliable narrators" and tricky points of view until near the end of the poetry unit; that makes a nice transition into the study of fiction or drama. I guess my approach is formal and technical, more or less without ideology, and based on the concerns authors themselves seem to have and the concerns creative writing teachers impart to their students: if the poet can achieve a singular, individual voice, then the poem seems alive. Ideology deadens poems more quickly than it deadens criticism, which is quickly indeed. The life in the poem's voice is worth any number of ideas.

The written assignment sheet for this paper would have the usual directions for a composition, such as length, form, and warnings about conventions and advice about revision and polish. In addition to promoting a three-part organization, I have often specified some works in the "Poems for Further Reading" section which I think they might find most helpful in illustrating tone and voice. I usually require that they choose one poem to write on from such a list as this: Elizabeth

Barrett Browning, "How do I love thee? Let me count the ways;" John Donne, "Death be not proud;" Thomas Hardy, "The Convergence of the Twain" and "Hap;" Gerard Manley Hopkins, "Spring and Fall;" A.E. Housman, "Loveliest of Trees" and "To an Athlete Dying Young;" Johnson, "On My First Son;" Pastan, "Ethics." I favor the neoclassical clarity of Housman, and the Hopkins poem is an interesting challenge in its tone. To follow up the initial lesson, I will usually teach, as I noted earlier, a dramatic monologue—Browning's "Soliloquy of the Spanish Cloister" and "My Last Duchess" are both in the book—and then progress to poems of complex tone, such as works by John Keats and Robert Frost (" 'Out, Out—' " works well), as well as "To His Coy Mistress," a Shakespeare sonnet (I favor "That time of year thou may'st in me behold"), and Henry Reed's marvelous bi-voiced "Naming of Parts." I like to close this part of the course by talking about William Blake's "The Tyger" with the class and trying to get them to discuss tone as an aspect of the poem which perhaps helps us understand the other aspects. That poem is always a challenge to us all.

By the time the class has spent a couple of weeks on voice and tone and has written once on a poem, I usually move them on to the units on diction and imagery, which I teach together. Once they have understood that a poetic voice may seem to say one thing but may mean another thing altogether, they are more ready for the sometimes surprising workings of imagery and symbolism than they otherwise would have been.

Writing Assignments on Poems

Writing Assignments on
W. H. Auden's "Musée des Beaux Arts"

Samuel Maio
SAN JOSE STATE UNIVERSITY
SAN JOSE, CALIFORNIA

One of the more elementary ways to use W. H. Auden's "Musée des Beaux Arts"in order to make a few points about composition is to get students to consider how the poem is structured like a good "theme" paper. This exercise is helpful in reinforcing some of the principal methods of organizing such a paper. The opening lines of the Auden poem can be read as a "thesis statement," even if it is one written with the poet having inverted the usual syntax for rhythmic effect and sound: "About suffering they were never wrong, / The Old Masters. . ." The ensuing lines in the first stanza can be read as the poet's refining his thesis by specifying how the Old Masters variously evoked the broad concept of suffering. The second stanza identifies and explains one specific work by a Master for illustration. Read in this way, the poem becomes the classic paradigm for basic paragraph structure, which, in turn, is the template for structuring any theme, thesis, or argument paper: part one, a statement of thesis or thematic intention or topic; part two, the amplification and further definition of that thesis, theme, or topic; and part three, an example offered as corroboration. The writing exercise should be about two to three pages long. Here are some questions to get students thinking: How would you rearrange the words of the poem's opening lines in order to make a conventionally prosaic thesis statement?

How might the poem be read as an essay? What kind of essay would you call it and why? What are the principal methods of organization used in this type of essay?

For segments of a composition course focused more on literature (such as those taught in the University of California system where the introduction to literature course also serves as a freshman-level composition course), a similar exercise can be used. Auden's poem can be regarded as a Petrarchan sonnet, though one not adhering to the form's traditional length, meter, or rhyme schemes. The poem is sonnet-like in its being a brief lyrical meditation on a single theme (suffering). Further, the poem is divided in two parts, moving from the general in the first stanza to the precise in the second. The division between these parts can be viewed as the *volta* (or "turn") found in the Petrarchan sonnet which marks the poem's turn towards its closure, synthesis, or resolution. Some questions to ask students are: What is the poem's rhyme pattern? What effects does this pattern have on the poem? How many times does Auden use the word "how" in the poem and to what effect(s)? How might the poem be read as a sonnet? What type of sonnet would you regard the poem as being, and why? After considering these questions, the student should be asked to compare and contrast, in three to four pages, Auden's poem with a traditional sonnet, such as Thomas Hardy's "Hap," which is a Petrarchan sonnet and is also a meditation on suffering.

A Two-Step Imitation:
Elizabeth Bishop's "The Fish"

Lee Upton
LAFAYETTE COLLEGE
EASTON, PENNSYLVANIA

Elizabeth Bishop's "The Fish"—so beautifully bent on the effects of re-envisioning—makes its own subtle argument for the sort of serious revision that we ask of our students. In working with "The Fish," it may be useful to ask students to write both an imitation of the poem and a revision of their first imitation, noting that they will revise their first imitation after we discuss Bishop's poem in some depth in class. First, they are to create an exploratory, generative imitation; that is, they must compose an imitation as a means for studying Bishop's poem and preparing for an in-depth classroom discussion of it. After our classroom discussion, they are to compose a second draft (or an entirely new imitation of "The Fish," should they wish) accompanied by a description (at least one page in length) of their processes in which they explain the decisions they made as they sought to duplicate Bishop's effects. For this exercise not only imitations but parodies are allowed ("And I ate the fish whole").

In the first draft of the imitation students are to pay special attention to the range of images that Bishop employs. They may begin by dramatically changing the tone of the original, perhaps by substituting another subject for Bishop's. To gain an initial sense of the poem's shape, students may find it helpful to count the syllables in each line of Bishop's poem. They might also want to note the ratio of monosyllabic to polysyllabic words. They should note the poem's particular sound effects and the use of simile and metaphor and the intervals between them. They might also be encouraged to pay attention to Bishop's punctuation, particularly her use of dashes, as these mark the fisher's attempts to focus more precisely on her catch.

To be sure, some first drafts are quite wonderful ("And I let the certified public accountant go"; "And I let my husband/wife go"). But a piece of writing that imitates some of the sophisticated visual adventures of the original, that allows for psychological and imagistic complexity, is called for in a revision. The second attempt—written after we have discussed as a group both the students' imitations and Bishop's poem—may make it possible for students to change their imitations dramatically.

After the first imitations are completed and read aloud in class, we discuss Bishop's poem in depth. At this point, some students already tend to have a laudable sense of partial ownership of "The Fish," of having participated from the inside out with the poem's dynamics. By creating an imitation, students have read and written with intensity, and, as a result, our classroom discussion of the poem's challenges and idiosyncracies may be more specific and more closely textured. In particular, students have had an opportunity through this sort of combination of emulation and active study to gain a greater awareness of the working of images, not simply as accumulations of details but as conceptual and emotional acts.

Just as the poem is devoted to moments of re-envisioning and re-questioning initial perceptions, so too during class discussion should we focus on taking another look at Bishop's poem. We might explore, for instance, the progression in meaning that Bishop's images make possible and that first drafts generally cannot accommodate. That is, together, we examine the fisher's peculiar manner of seeing as it affects her understanding.

Any somewhat close imitation of "The Fish" must hinge on a reversal of original intention, a moment of discovery that is revealed through the speaker's newly dazzled vision and her culminating action: "And I let the fish go." We must ask ourselves what images have led toward such an epiphanic moment. During discussion we focus on the ways in which the poem is more than a catalogue of details. Images of the fish inform us of the fisher's own identity, and of her way of seeing and of orienting herself in the world. Initially the fisher sees the fish as an object, focusing on its external appearance with a penetrating attention that overcomes revulsion as she notes the fish's "tiny white sea-lice." We then follow her movement inward, a nearly surgical invasiveness as she imagines the fish's interior, "the coarse white flesh / packed in like feathers" and "the pink swim-bladder / like a big peony." We note the distancing elements of her images, her focus on dissimilarity. For much of the poem she forgoes any note of similarity between herself and the fish. The fish's eyes do not "return" her "stare"; the fish's jaw works by means of a "mechanism." The speaker's distanced observation is only disrupted when she notes the fishhooks embedded in the fish's "lower lip." We may then plot out the fisher's remarkable shift in attitude as her descriptiveness makes the fish, in a dramatic turnabout, a source of complex wonder.

As students explore this turning point of the poem, it can be useful to ask them to write in class a response to the question: What motivates the speaker's perception of a "victory"? I have found it fruitful to ask students to overread, putting forward many potential answers. Some students might speculate, for instance, that the fisher's victory amounts to a celebration of her sportsmanship, of having bested the fish and other fishers. More frequently, students suggest that her vision is transformed (here we meet the most commonly accepted reading) by her awe in recognition of the fish as a valiant survivor and fighter. If we have spent class time with elements of Bishop's biography, responses might take another turn. It is a critical commonplace to think of Bishop as a poet preoccupied with questions about the nature of home. Essentially parentless, she was what her biographer, Brett C. Millier, calls "a chronically displaced person." Students might ask if the fish in this, her most anthologized poem, would seem to be mysteriously allied with the issue of home: the fish is described as "homely," and, early on, it is cast in domestic terms that link it to the faded walls of a home:

> his brown skin hung in strips
> like ancient wall-paper,
> and its pattern of darker brown
> was like wall-paper:
> shapes like full-blown roses
> stained and lost through age.

Students might ask if the fish represents a repressed desire for home, a desire that must now be "let go" by a speaker who is herself precariously poised, self-consciously out of her element in her "rented boat." Is the poem the release of a desire or an acknowledgment of a desire?

Certainly there is much else to discuss when working with "The Fish," and there's much else besides discussion that one can do during a class session devoted to "The Fish." Students might be asked to list images in the poem and categorize them according to the reference areas from which they emerge and the associations they evoke. Students can isolate "I" statements ("I caught"; "I thought"; "I looked"; "I admired"; "I saw"; "I stared and stared"; "And I let the fish go") and discuss the pattern of meaning that is created through them. They can experiment with revising the poem into the second or third person and writing an in-class response about the shifts in meaning and psychological distance that such changes impose.

As we closely examine Bishop's poem, students gain a new entry point into it, and the second stage of their assignment—writing a revision of their original imitation—creates a further challenge, for their revisions should attempt to accommodate some of the descriptive daring and psychological complexity of Bishop's poem.

While simply assigning one draft of an imitation can work quite well, there are advantages to the sort of two-step imitation that I am proposing. Students initially learn about the poem independently by attempting to copy some of its elements. At times unselfconscious acts of bold mimicry occur. Students may find that an imitation offers them both structure and within that structure the freedom of discovery. In turn, some students assume a poem must come to the poet "whole" and immediately or not at all, and they are intrigued by the exhilarating discipline that revision requires. Their second revision or version of an imitation may create a more sophisticated sensory response to their subject. And because the assignment works especially well as we study imagery, students may find that through their own revisions they gain a greater sense of the power of images and the associations to which images give rise.

Gathering:
Elizabeth Bishop's "Sestina"

~~~~~~

Terri Witek
STETSON UNIVERSITY
DeLAND, FLORIDA

To appreciate the mysteriousness and beauty of this poem, have the class read "Sestina" at home and ask that each person bring in an object that holds some sort of personal significance. They should not discuss their choices, and when they arrive in class with their objects they may not explain them, offer their histories, or even tell what they are, and no one may ask any questions. The objects should be gathered in the middle of the room where everyone can see them. When everyone has settled, ask each student to silently choose six objects and write a brief paragraph in which all six appear. Allot ten minutes to the task.

When everyone is finished, and rustling around in a self-congratulatory way, ask them to write a second, different paragraph in which the objects appear again. Allot ten more minutes.

Then the poll the room. Who chose which objects and why? Often the whole class will have found one or two objects so compelling that everyone uses them: what is it that has made that snow dome and that pencil sharpener seem essential? What objects didn't they choose? The discussion often elicits the point that Bishop's poem makes: that the most homely of objects (and note that she uses all nouns) are transformed into something rich and strange when they are put into the same space: the space of the room, the space of the poem. The sacredness of simple objects amounts to a belief system in the poetry of the last half of the twentieth century, you may point out. And add that since the endless recombination of such objects is one way of making of the everyday world a magic space, a sestina is a perfect example of the way this belief is matched with a form. What happened, for example, when they were forced into new combinations in their second paragraphs?

Now ask the students to read Bishop's poem aloud, a new voice for each stanza. Discuss the poem in light of what they have learned from their own experiments. Which, for example, are Bishop's most mysterious end words? Which are the hardest to reuse? What is the most amazing recombination? Which of her objects would they most like to have in our pile?

End class by having the students each read one of their own paragraphs out loud, one after another, so their texts can hook together in their own mysterious logic. Then each student collects an object and moves off into the rest of the day.

Writing Exercise for
Gary Gildner's "First Practice"

~~~~~~

Mark Sanders
COLLEGE OF THE MAINLAND
TEXAS CITY, TEXAS

A BRIEF OVERVIEW

We might read Gary Gildner's "First Practice" as a coming-of-age poem. Under the bullying guidance of Clifford Hill, a man who once served in the military and "killed / for his country," boys are not only taught how to play football and win the championship, but they are taught also that "dogs / ate dogs," and that when scrimmage lines form so does hate among friends. Anyone not agreeing with Clifford Hill's philosophy is a girl, not a man.

TOPICS FOR WRITING

1. Characterize Clifford Hill, examining how his attitude toward football and boys is shaped by extreme chauvinistic and militaristic attitudes. Having done this, compare or contrast Coach Hill to a coach you may have encountered during your schooling. Make an assessment of both coaches; that is, would you care to play for either one? Explain.

2. Philosophically, do you believe Coach Hill's methods are appropriate for the training of young athletes? Describe what you might anticipate in a standard practice with Coach Hill, and

discuss whether you think such a practice is beneficial for learning to play a particular sport.

3. In "First Practice," Gary Gildner describes the location for the practice as "under the grade school, / where we went in case of attack / or storm." These particular lines bear far more importance than might first be noted, but when we consider the connotations attached to the description we discover the gym is an underground shelter. Discuss what a shelter's purpose is and the irony of Hill's abuse—his "attack / or storm"—in such a location. Can you think of other shelters children have that ironically place them in abusive situations? Explain.

4. Frequently in American literature, the building has been used as a model for the psyche. Generally and simply speaking, the upstairs portions of buildings represent the activities or impulses of the Ego; what transpires on the staircases or elevators is a representation of Super-ego activities or impulses; and, what takes place beneath groundlevel, in the basement or cellar, is representative of Id activities or impulses. If we regard the grade school's basement as a psychological model of the Id, the children have been drawn to asocial and amoral depths in the very institution that pedagogically seeks to train them in Super-ego and Ego responses to daily living. Metaphorically, the children are taken to the basement to be trained in the dark impulses of humanity. Discuss what these dark impulses are as illustrated in the poem and how these do not align to morality and reason as taught in school.

"The Purpose of Poetry is to Tell Us about Life"

Ron Rash
TRI-COUNTY TECHNICAL COLLEGE
PENDLETON, SOUTH CAROLINA

In his chapbook *Fugue State*, Indiana poet Jared Carter states, "The purpose of poetry is to tell us about life." A poem that supports Carter's comment especially well is Robert Hayden's "Those Winter Sundays," and I have found this poem to be one that makes the connection between art and life clear to my freshman composition students. After discussing the child's indifference to his father's labors of love, I ask my students to recall similar moments from their own childhoods, moments when they were indifferent or only aware years later of "love's austere and lonely offices." Because some of my students have not grown up in a traditional family setting, I emphasize to my students that the adult does not have to be their biological father or mother; it can be anyone who raised or helped raise them. Almost always my students are quick to respond with examples from their own lives. The one time when no immediate personal anecdotes were forthcoming, I offered an example from my own life. When I finished my anecdote, I again asked the class for some examples, and several hands went up.

I have never had a class in which every student offers an example from his or her life. Some students are too shy or are uncomfortable discussing personal aspects of their lives in a classroom setting. For others, an example does not come immediately to mind. However, hearing examples from other students' lives triggers similar memories for the students who do not speak up in class. Furthermore, I offer to help students after class if they are still having trouble finding an example from their own lives. Perhaps I have been lucky, but I have never had a student who could not compare an event in his or her life to Hayden's poem.

At the end of the class period I give the actual assignment: an essay in which the student compares an experience in his or her own life to "Those Winter Sundays." Because there is sometimes a tendency for students to forget that the assignment is a comparison of a work of art to an event in their lives, not just an autobiographical essay, I emphasize that the body of the essay should discuss both the event in their lives *and* its similarity to the poem.

After completing this assignment, I believe my students have a better understanding of Jared Carter's comment.

Student Essay

~~~~~~

A FATHER'S LOVE

The moment I read Robert Hayden's "Those Winter Sundays," my mind went back to my own childhood. I remember well the bone-chilling winters in Detroit. I remember the snow and the joy I had playing in that winter wonderland. I also remember that even though my childhood was happy, there seemed to be a coldness in the home atmosphere as well. There was not a great deal of affection given. My father, in particular, seemed to be unable to show me the kind of affection and love that I needed. My young heart was unable to comprehend that Daddy was demonstrating his love for me by his sacrificial acts of kindness.

In my remembering, I cannot recall ever getting up on a frigid winter morning and finding the house cold. Just as Hayden's father rose early to stoke the fire, my father also got up well before the rest of the family. The furnace that had been turned down to a chilly fifty-five degrees during the night was turned back up to a comfortable seventy degrees by the time I got out of bed.

I do not remember ever thanking my father for performing that act of kindness. It was a sacrifice for him because he hates the cold. He is extremely thin, and the cold goes right to his bones. Even so, he was willing to get up in the cold so the rest of us could be warm. Daddy told me that he enjoyed rising early. He said he liked the quiet and the solitude. As a six-year-old would, I believed him. Now, as an adult, I see that excuse as another proof of his love. He did not want me to feel sorry for him. He wanted to remove any feelings of guilt that I might have for not being thankful.

Hayden also mentions that his good shoes were polished for Sunday. I, too, often found my Sunday shoes shined and ready for me to wear to church. Daddy's hands, tired and painful from welding burns, carefully and lovingly cleaned my shoes.

I was longing for hugs and kisses and silly times because that was the way all the daddies in the storybooks acted. However, all I usually received was a quick kiss on the forehead at bedtime. Today I treasure the memory of those little kisses because I know how difficult it was for Daddy to show affection.

Now that I am forty-two and Daddy is seventy-two, I realize those little sacrifices were his way of saying, "I love you, Curly." Not long ago Daddy came to visit for a few days. Each morning he slept in until well after nine o'clock! At first I thought he must be sick, but then it dawned on me. My husband had risen early, turned up the heat pump, and had a warm crackling fire in the fireplace. Daddy did not have to sacrifice for me anymore. He had passed that torch to my husband many years ago. Now he can sleep in until the house is warm. He can warm those loving hands by the fire anytime. At the end of "Those Winter Sundays," Hayden laments, "What did I know, what did I know of love's austere and lonely offices?" I, too, can cry out, "I did not know." But now I know, and it is not too late to tell him.

Dramatic Situation and the Uses of Induction

~~~~~~

R.S. Gwynn
LAMAR UNIVERSITY
BEAUMONT, TEXAS

We hear a great deal these days about such matters as the "indeterminacy" of poems and the error of instructors' attempting to impose their own interpretations on literary texts. I do not wish to get into arguments about the uses and abuses of current literary theory in the classroom, but I must assert that occasionally it is the instructor's responsibility to exercise his or her authority as a trained reader of poems and to reject some of the readings students come up with. A poem should not be turned into a *tabula rasa* on which students are allowed to scrawl purely subjective responses which have little or nothing to do with the text at hand. In student writing, gross misreadings of poems may occur if students have not been taught to ask basic questions about a poem's dramatic situation and to determine the answers to this question: "*Who* is saying *what* to *whom* under *what circumstances*?" Since students must work with tiny hints and clues in the poems, they must apply the inductive method to establish the basis upon which all other matters of interpretation must rest.

For a writing assignment on poetry, I favor using three or four short poems, each usually under ten lines, for an assignment which is usually titled something like "Different Types of Dramatic Situation." I usually select several poems from *Literature* and distribute copies of others from the public domain. Some of my favorites include A.E. Housman's "Eight O'Clock," Walter Savage Landor's "Mother, I Cannot Mind My Wheel," Robert Louis Stevenson's "Requiem," Countee Cullen's "Incident" or

"For a Lady I Know," and Cleghorn's "The Golf Links." These are all traditional poems written in simple language, and the list contains examples of lyric, narrative, and dramatic poetry. In some of them the speaker seems to be the poet; in others, an invented character or omniscient narrator. Landor's poem has a named auditor. "Eight O'Clock" and "The Golf Links," to mention two, have clearly defined settings, and time is important in both Housman's poem and Cullen's "Incident." Of course, there are many other poems that may be used for this assignment, even longer ones, but the instructor should take care to select poems with a variety of speakers, auditors, and sets of circumstances.

Practice on similar poems, and a day or so of in-class preparation (discussion groups are especially valuable here) are useful for this assignment. It is important to stress that some matters of interpretation (if we can call them that) are really not open to much debate. "Eight O'Clock," for example, is not about a harried businessman who is troubled by a too-tight seatbelt while stuck in a traffic jam on the way to his downtown office; it is about a convicted man with a noose around his neck—no more, no less. It is true that we do not know the exact nature of his crime or even whether he feels any remorse about it—these things *are* debatable and may be legitimately asked. For example, does "cursed his luck" mean that the criminal remains unrepentant? In writing about these poems, students who do not look carefully at virtually every word in each poem will go astray; many have glossed over the crucial "noosed" in "Eight O'Clock" and, thus, do not recognize the impending execution. In Countee Cullen's "For a Lady I Know," misdefining "class" might lead them to assume that the title character is a schoolteacher when, in fact, Cullen means "class" in the social sense. Not thinking of the historical meaning of "wheel" in Landor's little masterpiece can also result in misidentifying the setting, and failure to look closely at the verb tenses in the same poem might result in students' not understanding that the young woman's love has proven inconstant. If students can master techniques here, in fairly accessible poems that can be discussed in compact paragraphs, then they should be able to apply the same inductive methods of reading to the more complicated poems and interpretive matters that they will encounter later in the course.

Using Langston Hughes's "Theme for English B" to Help Students Develop Awareness of the Author/Audience Relationship

~~~~~~

William L. Scurrah
PIMA COMMUNITY COLLEGE
TUCSON, ARIZONA

Composition instructors often confront students who are reluctant, even afraid, to write. When such students say that they know what they want to say but don't know how to say it or that they suffer from writer's block, what they may in fact be telling us is that they don't know how to say what they want to say *to us*. Helping students to see their instructors as an audience, not just as judges, will open up the writing experience for them in new and creative ways. Langston Hughes's poem "Theme for English B" is the perfect vehicle for developing such awareness in our composition students, for in it he confronts the same dilemmas as they do whenever they are assigned to write an essay.

The poem begins with the assignment: "Go home and write / a page tonight. / And let that page come out of you— / Then, it will be true." These are fairly typical instructions, and to an instructor, seemingly not only innocuous, but open-ended, encouraging the students to a degree of freedom. But as Hughes goes on to itemize, the assignment is fraught with dangers; it raises two kinds of questions in the student's mind: 1) What does "come out of you" mean? Is it really what the instructor wants? Do I really want to reveal so much of myself to a stranger? 2) How safe is it to be truthful? What is "truth" in this situation? How do I state my truth so my instructor understands and accepts it *as* true? No wonder Hughes says "I wonder if it's that simple?" and no wonder we get students crowding around us after class, asking for more specific guidance: What should we write about? Is it all right to do this? Or that? Should I write about current events? Can I write about my dog? And so on.

Students are aware that the assignment is not "that simple" and that their grade depends upon how they answer the questions the assignment raises. Fortunately, Hughes's poem provides some answers having to do with the crucial author/audience relationship. A reading and class discussion of the poem should therefore help students address and resolve the conflicts they confront whenever they have to write a college essay.

The poem may be assigned for overnight reading or presented unannounced in class the day you plan to assign an essay (the personal essay would work best for this, although the principles apply to any). Read the poem aloud and then invite general response. Because this poem deals directly with an immediate concern of the students, responses are likely to be numerous and varied; of course, they will include comments of Hughes's dilemmas as a black student with a white instructor and on how he attempts to resolve that conflict by claiming their shared Americanness, but as discussion progresses and is prompted by the instructor, students will also begin to reveal their identification with the poet's experience as an English student like themselves. The discussion can then be directed toward discovering how Hughes resolved the problems inherent in the assignment.

First, Hughes give a bare-bones biography, where he lives, how old he is, and so forth, establishing the physical distance or difference between himself and his instructor. Thus he demonstrates that where one comes from acts as a point of beginning for the essay: "I take the elevator / up to my room, sit down, and write this page:". The colon at the end of the stanza signals a beginning, a beginning from a physical reality of age, ethnicity, neighborhood, economic circumstance, etc. He is not a disembodied ideal student but has a real, experienced, describable existence—as do each of our students in our classes. (To facilitate students' use of personal biography as the starting point for thinking about the author/audience dialogue, the instructor might present a brief oral autobiography, thus beginning the process of making the students think about him/her as a human being who can be addressed, as an audience not as a judge.) Then, Hughes attempts to itemize the points of connection and measure the areas of difference between himself and his instructor: "you, me, talk on this page" about age, place, race, tastes, relative freedom, and so forth. When he says "Sometimes perhaps you don't want to be a part of me. / Nor do I often want to be a part of you," he may resonate with students who often do not want to be in an English class and do not know why they have to be there, and when he says, "But we are, that's true!" he underlines that through the writing of an essay, a student can establish a connection with his/her audience.

After general class discussion, assign students to write an essay of about five hundred words modeled after or inspired by Hughes's poem in which they address the issues he raises from their own points of view: How do they approach writing assignments? How do they resolve the conflicts any college writing assignment creates? What authorial stance do they take vis-à-vis their instructor? What do they assume an instructor wants and how do they reconcile that with what they want to write? Follow description of the assignment with a short period (twenty minutes) of small groups during which students can discuss among themselves their experiences and fears of writing, especially in terms of author/audience relationships.

The purpose of this exercise is to cultivate in students a consciousness of the dynamics involved in the relationship between an author and his/her audience, especially to help them realize the value of establishing their identities in their essay writing and not to lose themselves behind a facade of artificial objectivity sometimes so extreme that their essays seem written by "Anonymous." Offering Hughes's poem as a model will help students see themselves in a new way, as authors with something to say to an audience: "As I learn from you, / I guess you learn from me—."

Examining Alliteration and Assonance in Open-Form Poems

~~~~~~

Joseph Green
LOWER COLUMBIA COLLEGE
LONGVIEW, WASHINGTON

Because they've grown up with it and continue to live with it in popular music, whether they enjoy reading poetry or not, my students never have any trouble recognizing exact rhyme, especially end rhyme; however, they sometimes resist the notion of slant rhyme and find all but the most obvious use of alliteration and assonance downright elusive. In the chapter "Sound," the examples that X. J. Kennedy and Dana Gioia use to illustrate assonance and alliteration are mainly closed-form poems with rhymed line endings. While they do comment further on sound in their chapter "Open Form," they don't give it much analysis there.

To observe the repetition of sounds in a poem, I always have to say the words aloud, feel them, polish them on the tongue. For me, this is one of the great pleasures of reading poetry, and the rewards are especially satisfying when they surprise me, when sound effects are not reinforced by an obvious rhyme scheme or rhythmical pattern. Consequently, the first objective of this assignment is to draw students directly into that same experience: reading open-form poems aloud for the sake of their sound.

For example, take a look at the first four lines of "Men at Forty," by Donald Justice:

Men at forty
Learn to close softly
The doors to rooms they will not be
Coming back to.

If you read the lines aloud, pacing them, pronouncing the words roundly, you'll *feel* the sounds as much as hear them. "Learn" recalls "Men." "Doors" recalls "forty," and in a different manner, perhaps somewhat less obviously, "close." At the end of the second and third lines, "not be" rhymes with "softly." And at the end of the fourth line, "to" calls back to "rooms." The sounds of consonants and vowels braid the lines together.

The rest of the poem is equally rich in sound, sometimes with obvious effect—"stair" mirroring "rest" in the first line of the next stanza, and later "lather" echoing "father"—and sometimes more subtly. By the time you reach the end of the poem, you're ready for the last word, "houses," to close (softly, of course) with a recollection of "sound" from the first line of the final stanza and "now" from the stanza before.

When students follow this process, reading aloud, examining the repetition of consonant vowel sounds, they very quickly reach an understanding of alliteration and assonance, and they start to feel the music of language in open-form poems, where they may have thought before that it was missing. Still, a poem like "Men at Forty" is much more than a collection of sounds, so the assignment's second objective is to move students toward analyzing the connection between sound, structure, and sense.

I usually provide a list of poems, good candidates for aural analysis. This limits the potential difficulties somewhat, keeps the discussion focused on open-form poems, and creates automatic working groups among students. I select different poems from time to time, just to keep myself fresh, but some favorites include Robert Hayden's "Those Winter Sundays," Theodore Roethke's "Root Cellar," Alice Fulton's "What I Like," and, of course, Donald Justice's "Men at Forty."

Students read all of the poems on the list, and then select one to examine in a short essay. They practice saying the poem they have chosen, trying to feel it as they speak, writing down the sounds and the words that connect them, more or less in the manner that I moved through the first stanza of "Men at Forty." The next step—making a statement about the use of sound, the effect of it in the poem—can be the hardest part for some students, but because it forms a thesis for the essay, it is a crucial step. I like to have students work in small groups at this point, helping one another to hear the poems, raising questions, and offering suggestions, until they have a sense of what they want to say in their essays. Often they discover various ways in which sound can reinforce imagery or meaning in a poem. Then they're really onto something.

I generally ask students to present their papers, saying the poems aloud, and sharing their ideas with the whole class in a roundtable discussion, before they attempt their final drafts. This allows them to say things that aren't quite safe or completely tested, and it gives them an opportunity to ask questions of their audience. Many essays go through dramatic changes as a result of these sessions. Final drafts, typed and double-spaced, are usually about three pages long.

This assignment has worked especially well for me in introductory poetry classes, but it can also be effective in composition courses. I like to introduce it with this quote from Richard Hugo: "When I was a young poet, I set an arbitrary rule that when I made a sound I felt was strong, a sound I liked specially [sic], I'd make a similar sound three to eight syllables later. Of course it would often be a slant rhyme. Why three to eight? Don't ask. You have to be silly to write poems at all."[1] By the end of the assignment, students will usually have a sense of why Hugo would set such a rule for himself—and most of them don't think it's silly.

Notes

1. Hugo, Richard. 1979. *The Triggering Town*. New York: Norton.

Letting Go:
Robert Lowell's "Skunk Hour"

~~~~~~

Terri Witek
STETSON UNIVERSITY
DE LAND, FLORIDA

Teach this poem directly after Elizabeth Bishop's "Sestina," pointing out ahead of time that Lowell and Bishop were very good friends and admired each other's work. Tell the class that in several earlier versions of "Skunk Hour" the poem was not only dedicated to Bishop, but that she seemed to be riding around in one of the "love cars" with him, and in one version they seem to have a crying baby. In another version the persona addresses the man in the moon. The point is that a lot of things that used to be gathered in the drafts of "Skunk Hour" have disappeared in the final version.

Ask the students to read the poem, then come to class with two paragraphs in which they have written a story that includes a specific setting, several minor characters, a relationship between the narrator and someone else, at least two pieces of overheard language, and at least two declarative statements. In class, ask them to eliminate at least half of what they've brought in by crossing out sentences. Then they should cross out inessential words in the sentences. Now ask them to line up what remains on a new sheet of paper, rearranging the elements if they wish. When they feel they are finished, tell them they must take one object from the last class and confront it in at least two new lines at the end. Now read the Lowell poem aloud and ask the students what their own work has taught them about it.

The beginning of this exercise demonstrates that making objects disappear from a space can be as mysteriously productive as gathering them: Bishop and Lowell use quite different techniques to similar ends in "Sestina" and "Skunk Hour." Oddly enough, both poems offer worlds that are filled with objects and yet from which things seem to be missing: not only the objects but the spaces between them, then, resonate with meaning. What the students have taken out of their writing is as important as the repressed histories and explanations of the objects they brought into class during the "Sestina" discussion. This suggests that, to latter-day twentieth-century poets like Lowell and Bishop, both what fills a space and what it lacks are ways of telling the story of the essential mysteriousness of the world.

Of course the most perverse part of the exercise is what happens at the end, when the students are forced to include an object from another place. But that's what Lowell did by adding in a skunk after all his deletions, and it's the final triumph of his poem. (It's also a way of dedicating our efforts to Bishop, too.) The move reminds us that one new element has the power to alter a space forever: each new object invades our domesticated landscapes much like Lowell's mother skunk invades his garbage pail. While there is something scary about this, there is something wonderful in the world's determination to break into even our most protected spaces. Have the students read their revised work aloud and prove the point: inevitably, they like the last parts best.

Making Decisions About
Values And Ethics

~~~~~~

David McCracken
TEXAS A & M UNIVERSITY

During the semesters that I have taught English: Introduction to Literature, one assignment seems to evoke more energetic, insightful, personal responses from students than any other, and although it relates to more than one poem, the exercise asks students to focus on one question that is pertinent to their study of literature.

When I assign students to read the chapter "Listening to a Voice," I ask them to pay special attention to several of the canonical works such as Williams's "The Red Wheelbarrow," Auden's "The Unknown Citizen," Owen's "Dulce et Decorum Est," and Blake's "The Chimney Sweeper." Most of the students in the class have taken AP English courses during high school and have read the poems; however, almost none of them have been exposed to Bettie Sellers's "In the Counselor's Waiting Room." As a result, I ask my students to be prepared to discuss Sellers's poem and also Linda Pastan's "Ethics," and then to write a response in their journals to this question: "Without extensively experiencing the world outside of the classroom, are people well prepared enough to make effective decisions about values or ethics?"

My teaching objectives in an introductory literature course are to expose students to the various genres, to help them to understand literary techniques, and to show them how to unveil the deeper meanings in the texts. I stress writing as well as reading during the course, and besides several short essays and an exam, I ask students to keep a journal in which they react personally to the literature. Sometimes I will tell the students that we will discus their entries during class and not to be afraid to bring their own frames of reference to bear upon the literature. Doing this often creates interpretations with which I nor your editors agree. When explicating Roethke's "My Papa's Waltz," I agree with you that the poem's rhythm is "rollicking" and I visualize a touching scene affectionately remembered by the speaker, but when students interpret the work as the persona's recollection of an alcoholic father and a co-dependant mother, I will not say that their interpretation is wrong if they are thorough in their discussion. (I once gave this poem to a physician who coordinated an alcohol and drug rehabilitation program and spent hours refuting his interpretation that the poem is about substance abuse.)

When I teach the chapter about voice, I will select one of the assigned poems and demonstrate how an analysis of the speaker's tone helps us to understand the overall meaning of the text. When students begin to discuss "In the Counselor's Waiting Room," they usually summarize that there is a young woman attending a psychology course whose mother has asked her to see one of the college counselors because she has begun to reject her parents' values, especially concerning family and home. When they begin to investigate how irony illuminates the poem's meaning, several students interpret the poem as your editors do in the instructor's manual, that it is ironic that the earthy "terra cotta girl," product of her "home soil," does not appear to have the same proclivity for procreation as the previous generations of women in her family. However, after this the discussion may take several turns. Several students will often question the irony of the farm girl attending college and reading about existentialism, some will defend that the enlightened girl has a right to make her own decisions, others will argue that one psychology class does not provide enough worldly knowledge for the girl to disobey her family. At some point, students question what is meant by "finds no ease there / from the guilt of loving / the quiet girl down the hall." Contrary to what your editors consider as perhaps reading too much into the poem, many students interpret the work as one about sexual repression. They may begin questioning Sellers's selections of "existentialism," "psychology," and "Baptist," and when they do I write on the board their connotations of each word and I keep a dictionary handy so we can compare them to their denotations.

This progression of events has occurred in each of the introduction to literature classes that I have taught, and when students begin to examine the social implications of the poem, I ask them to explain to me the relationship between the "terra cotta girl" and her mother and to determine the conflicting values between them. This is usually when the quietest students in the class express themselves. They may argue that the "home soil" has no right to ask the girl to visit the counselor, that the poem illustrates the negative stereotype of women as only breeder, and that the girl should be able to make her own sexual and social decisions. If the discussion has reached this point, I ask the class to shift to "Ethics." On the board, I list their perceptions of ethics and then offer them a standard definition, usually citing that it is a code of morals of a particular person, religion, group, or profession. I then ask the students to describe the speaker's tone in the first part of the poem, and I particularly listen to how they respond to the academic setting in which Linda replies that the woman should make the decision whether or not to be saved.

When we discuss the second section of the work, I ask the students if there is a tone shift and what perhaps has caused the change. I then ask them to notice how the last six and a half lines relate to some of the descriptions in Sellers's poem. I point out "the browns of the earth" that the now elderly speaker sees in the painting and how she now realizes that the "woman / and painting and season are almost one / and all beyond saving by children" corresponds to the earth images and the young woman, redirecting the students back to their initial journal question: "Without extensively experiencing the world outside of the classroom, are people well prepared enough to make effective decisions about values or ethics?"

Obviously, each class is different and students will respond in other ways than the ones that I have mentioned. If there is not enough class time to complete this exercise, I will go over "Tone" and "In the Counselor's Waiting Room," and because most of the journal entries will react to "Ethics," I will respond to their impressions through my comments.

Revision and Meaning:
Ezra Pound's "In a Station of the Metro"

~~~~~~

David J. Rothman
CRESTED BUTTE ACADEMY
CRESTED BUTTE, COLORADO

The French poet Paul Valéry once made a comment to the effect that poems are never finished, only abandoned. We tend to think that this abandoning happens when a poet publishes his or her work—but that is not always the case. Many of the most powerful poems have been revised—sometimes repeatedly—after they have already been published, and they exist in several public versions. Among others, Walt Whitman and W. H. Auden are particularly well-known for having revised work that had already appeared; to cite another kind of example, there are more than fifty manuscripts of William Langland's fourteenth-century poem *Piers Plowman*, many of which were heavily edited by scribes over a long period of time, and which are very different from each other.

We know that when Ezra Pound was working on "In a Station of the Metro" in the early 1910s, he was experimenting with different techniques in an attempt to create a truly modern poetry. What most readers don't realize is that this famous poem, which is often taken as a breakthrough to the techniques of Imagism and High Modernism, looked quite different in later, book versions than when it first appeared in *Poetry* magazine in 1913. In later versions, the poem looks like this:

> The apparition of these faces in the crowd;
> Petals on a wet, black bough.

But in the *Poetry* version, the one first published, the poem looks something like this:

> The apparition   of these faces   in the crowd :
> Petals   on a wet, black   bough .

Pound's revisions are particularly fascinating, as they involve not a single change to any word in the poem—yet when we look at the two versions, they seem quite different, in a number of ways.

In your essay, describe the changes that Pound made to his poem, then speculate as to why he might have made them. What is added to the poem by the changes? What is lost? What remains unchanged (if anything)? Do Pound's changes indicate different cues for performance, or do they have significance in and of themselves as unperformable qualities of the poem's meaning? (How does one perform the extra space before a period in the original version, for example?) Or can the revision involve both of these kinds of changes at the same time? On a larger level—why, in his search for what is "modern," do you think Pound might have revised his little poem to look more conventional on the page? Which version do you think is more successful (if either)?

Remember, as you write, that well-organized speculation is as powerful as any conclusion you might reach. This question of poetic craft is profound and confusing: entertain the possibilities.

Writing Exercise for
Anne Sexton's "Her Kind"

~~~~~~

Mark Sanders
COLLEGE OF THE MAINLAND
TEXAS CITY, TEXAS

A BRIEF OVERVIEW

Anne Sexton's "Her Kind" is a bitter examination of womanhood. The poem illustrates a sisterhood of women who are "possessed" witches, "braver at night," and "dreaming evil." Sexton describes a woman as a "lonely thing, twelve-fingered, out of mind," "not a woman, quite." Suburban homes are "warm caves in the woods," and husbands and children are worms and elves. Additionally, Sexton alludes to lovers as being like Pluto, the Greek god of the underworld. Abducted and seduced, the woman as Persephone waves good-bye to villages along "the last bright routes," is consumed and bitten by Pluto's hellish passions, and is ultimately crushed under his wheels. Consequently, "a woman like that is not ashamed to die."

TOPICS FOR WRITING

1. "Her Kind" shows the disparity between actual womanhood and ideal womanhood. A woman, as described by Sexton, is "not a woman, quite." Contrast Sexton's illustration of womanhood to what you perceive as ideal womanhood. In other words, what will it take to make a woman a woman?
2. Trying to overlook Sexton's own suicide, concentrate on the last two lines. The poem's apparent nihilism suggests that

death is sometimes a preferred alternative to life. What in the poem illustrates that life is so unsatisfactory to women that they should not feel shame in choosing death? Additionally, while this may be a disquieting thought, what in your own existence would make death a preferred alternative to life? Or, what in even the most unhappy of existences keeps life sacred?

3. Think about women you know. How well do they fit Sexton's descriptions? Do you know a woman who is "out of mind"? How did she get that way? Do you know a woman who is "braver at night"? What necessitates her inhibitions? Look at each of Sexton's descriptions and draw parallels to women you know.

4. If "Her Kind" depicts womanhood, it also depicts manhood. According to Sexton's implications, what are men like? How are they worms and devils; what, along with their elfish children, do they whine about and "disalign"; how do they make women lonely? How do they make women want to die?

Writing Exercise for
Karl Shapiro's "The Dirty Word"

~~~~~~

Mark Sanders
COLLEGE OF THE MAINLAND
TEXAS CITY, TEXAS

A BRIEF OVERVIEW

Karl Shapiro's "The Dirty Word" examines how language sometimes has power over us and how it possesses us. The small boy who "bears the big bird of the dirty word into the house" is not only terrified of the word but "delights" in its excrement. Terrible and savagely beautiful, the dirty word rages in the cage and closet of the boy's mind and feeds upon his brain. However, the dirty word wishes to "escape from the zoo of the vocabulary," as if the word should not be separated from normal, respectable language. Only when the boy grows old and dies is the caged word released.

The narrator imposes how he has murdered the dirty word and how he has fashioned pens from its feathers to write elegies. While the word never truly escaped the "zoo of the vocabulary," because it is a dead word now, it no longer possesses the power it once had. Unlike the boy, the narrator who kills the word has power over language; he himself is free to use language as he desires.

TOPICS FOR WRITING:

1. Think of the occasions when you, as a youngster, learned "dirty" words. Describe the occasion when the words became part of your "vocabulary zoo," how you kept the words secret

in your home, how they possessed you, and how you used them either to hurt others or during inappropriate times. Describe as well the results of your use of these words. Are the dirty words of your youth still part of your adult vocabulary? Why or why not?

2. The boy who holds the word in his head until his death in old age represses the use of the dirty word. Society, or culture perhaps, forbids the use of the word. What words are forbidden to you? Why are these words taboo and what criteria determines their unacceptability? Do you impose the restrictions, or does some other censoring agency? Explain.

3. The adage states, "Sticks and stones may break my bones but words will never hurt me." Obviously, this statement is grossly untrue. Words hurt us, and any word or phrase that wounds us may fall into Shapiro's "zoo" of dirty words. Write about words that have hurt you, and explain why the words hurt.

4. "The Dirty Word" suggests that words may be killed; figuratively, they lose their original savagery. What words can you think of that once carried power, either positive or negative, and have lost significance? Discuss the original meaning of these words and what they mean today. In responding, you may want to consider politically correct speech.

5. Although Shapiro suggests that words lose their savagery over time, some words lose their innocence. For example, *hussy* once was a term of endearment, a pet name that meant "house wife." Now the word connotes a woman who practices unwholesomeness. Discuss other words that have lost their innocence and how that innocence was lost.

6. Dirty words include obscenities or profanities. In simple definition, obscenities are words that have to do with bodily functions or bodily parts; profanities target religion or deities. Argue either against the use of such words or defend their use.

For Tennyson's "Ulysses"

Fred Dings
WEST CHESTER UNIVERSITY
WEST CHESTER, PENNSYLVANIA

ASSIGNMENT FOR COMPOSITION

Write an essay which examines and compares the version or "reading" of Ulysses in Tennyson's poem to an earlier or more recent depiction. Be sure to discuss the similarities and differences of each version and explain how the versions are representative of the time in which they were written. In all cases, you might want to consider to what extent Tennyson's Ulysses is or is not representative of our time. Be sure to compare, analyze, and argue in your paper.

ASSIGNMENT FOR POETRY

Write a poem in the first person or third person in which you feature Ulysses or any other figure from classical mythology, such as Greek, Roman, or Judeo-Christian. Use a contemporary voice, and make decisions about rhythm, rhyme, diction, texture, images, and metaphors within the context of this particular project. In other words, try to make the form and content of your poem mutually responsive. You might consider the figure in some new situation, a contemporary one, or in a particular attitude, mood, or predisposition, Your poem might reveal some new way of thinking about the figure or our times.

COMMENTARY

One of the advantages of using Tennyson's poem as a focal point is not only its kinship with our modern sensibility, but its revisionary relationship to a literary tradition about which most students know little. Because we are working with poetry, a lecture including the versions of Ulysses found in Homer, Dante, Tennyson, and, possibly, Wallace Stevens can provide an overview of a tradition in less than one hour, even with students who have read none of the poems. This can be done entirely by lecture with a reading of selected passages in class or else with advanced reading of selected passages placed on reserve in the library. An assignment of this nature increases students' sense of their relationship to literary tradition and requires them to think and write comparatively.

In preparation for this assignment, I always spend time discussing the tradition of poetry featuring Ulysses, how Tennyson's poem fits into and adds to this tradition, and why this type of poem continues to be written. The extent to which I discuss these things depends on the level and nature of the course.

To begin, I review the characterization of Ulysses in Homer and Dante. First, I highlight the different characterizations we get of Odysseus (Ulysses) even in Homer, depending on whether we are reading the *Iliad* or the *Odyssey*, two texts which offer competing traditions. In particular, I will focus on certain passages in each text. In Book IX of the *Iliad*, we find Odysseus acting as an emissary to Akhilleus to rejoin the battle and save the ships from burning. Odysseus is known for his cleverness and craft in this tradition; since the text is celebrating the physical prowess and force of Akhilleus in competition with the craft of Odysseus, Odysseus is featured as a supplicant and told by Akhilleus to go and *think* of a way to save the ships without the power of Akhilleus, a power which of course becomes vitally necessary. In the *Odyssey*, Odysseus' talents are stressed over those of Akhilleus. In Book XI, we find Odysseus summoning the underworld and talking to the shade of Akhilleus. Here, in this competing tradition, we hear Akhilleus pronounce his own error in sacrificing his life for immortal fame, tacitly acknowledging Odysseus' way

as that best virtue which defeats death. Unless I am teaching a literature course, I seldom develop the discussion further than this.

Next, if there is time, I briefly discuss the characterization of
Ulysses (Odysseus) in Virgil as a "man of iron" and how Aeneas himself
is in part an Ulyssean figure. Normally, however, I move directly on to
Dante's placement of Ulysses in the eighth level of hell for being a
fraudulent counselor, for convincing his men to pursue knowledge and
new experiences in the world instead of pursuing knowledge of Christian love. In Canto XXVI, we find Ulysses portrayed as one "horn" of
a two-horned flame; the flame is described as "a tongue that tried to
speak" (Mandelbaum l. 89). The flame, figured as both a horn and a
tongue, is also then the language of Ulysses that goaded others along
with himself to eternal damnation. (This is a good time to further
underscore the value and working of the poetic image.)

I now lead directly into Tennyson's poem and discuss how
Ulysses' heroic quest for knowledge is not only redeemed, but redemp-
tive as he copes with declining powers in old age. The meter, blank
verse, is of course the meter of such English epics as John Milton's
Paradise Lost and William Wordsworth's *The Prelude*. The connections
here with the tradition should be apparent, but they might be stressed
anyway. As a class, we already will have read and discussed the overall
poem, but now I will focus on the heroic quest for knowledge featured
in lines such as 6-7, 31-32, 50-54, and 65-70. The main point to make
here in terms of the tradition is how Tennyson takes the figure of
Ulysses and features him as an exemplar of modern "scientific" man.
In a time when orthodox Christianity is less influential as a world view
than it once might have been, Tennyson's *reading* of Ulysses revises
Dante's and reflects the dominant values and attitudes of our time just
as Dante's reading reflected the dominant Christian world view of his
time. In addition, the tradition and character of Ulysses helps us read
ourselves and our relationship to the part in some new way. This, you
might stress, is one of the great values of being knowledgeable of our
literary traditions.

At this point, a thoughtful student might suggest that Tennyson's
view of Ulysses is no longer of our time. This would be an ideal time
to encourage that student to write an essay that argues that point. If I

have enough time, I include a reading of Stevens' "The Sail of Ulysses" and a few contemporary poems to bring the discussion to the nearly literal present. I also point out that this sort of chronological reading can be done with several major mythological figures. Also, since one problem that sometimes occurs in the poetry writing assignment is a student's too-loose identification with Tennyson's voice, I will bring in Louise Glück's "Aphrodite" or Mark Strand's "Orpheus Alone" as examples of other voices and interpretations of other mythological figures.

In closing, reading and writing in conscious relationship to our literary traditions is something which, among other things, I encourage. In a composition class, the organization, articulation, and analysis of ideas can in this case also lead to a greater appreciation of our poetic and mythological traditions.

Details:
A Writing Exercise

~~~~~~

Madeleine Mysko
JOHNS HOPKINS UNIVERSITY
BALTIMORE, MARYLAND

I have used the following writing assignment to reinforce the lesson that strong writing is characterized by the efficient handling of details. In preparation, I choose a character the class has encountered in the assigned readings. Particularly useful for this writing assignment are characters who have a "history" in the community or family, and whose changes over time have been observed (as opposed to revealed omnisciently or through that character's own first-person narration)—in fiction, for example, William Faulkner's Miss Emily ("A Rose for Emily") and James Baldwin's Sonny ("Sonny's Blues"); in poetry, Gwendolyn Brooks's Cousin Vit ("Rites for Cousin Vit"), Edwin Arlington Robinson's "Miniver Cheevy," and John Updike's Flick Webb ("Ex-Basketball Player").

I then write, and duplicate as a handout, a rather boring (but blessedly short) paragraph about that character, keeping the paragraph well above its subject, padding liberally with generalizations or abstractions, and avoiding particulars. For an example I have chosen Updike's Flick Webb:

> Flick Webb, who is employed at a local garage, is a familiar character in town. Although he has a lot of athletic potential and was once a promising member of his high school basketball team, Flick now appears to be unmotivated. When he is not at the garage, Flick seeks his relaxation in a nearby restaurant. He is a disappointment to those who remember his former accomplishments.

For this writing assignment I find I need a full class period, devoted half to discussion and half to in-class writing exercise.

I begin the discussion by reading "Ex-Basketball Player," followed by the paragraph I wrote about Flick. I point out the obvious: that while my paragraph presents the same Flick Webb, the picture isn't sharp at all, not only because clichés like "athletic potential" are always fuzzy, but also because details have been stripped from the exposition. By returning to the poem the class can then (either in small groups, or as a whole with someone recording at the blackboard) compile a list of specific details Updike provides. The list looks something like this:

- names of people and places ("Pearl Avenue" and "Mae")
- setting: the exact location of Berth's Garage, even the direction it faces; description of the pumps; description of Mae's luncheonette
- Flick's exact record: 390 points
- description of Flick's hands
- the names of real things: *lugwrench, inner tube, pinball, Necco Wafers*

The list could be much longer, of course.

Once, I attempted a short, in-class writing exercise in which students were to write a coherent paragraph or two from the above details. I found, alas, that the exercise was not so easy. The students were writing at a distance from their subject—a character about whom they had only second-hand information and feelings. Moreover, it proved defeating: after all, everybody could see before we started that a paragraph about Flick Webb couldn't hold a candle to Updike's poem, so why bother?

But listing details about Flick Webb, on the blackboard or in small-group discussion, does provide an excellent example of the sort of list-making one might do before writing the personal essay. Thus, during the remaining class time, I now ask my students to take a few minutes to choose a character they know well, but not intimately, as the speaker of "Ex-Basketball Player" knows Flick well, but not intimately.

Some suggestions are:

- an elderly relative
- someone your age, not necessarily a friend, whom you remember from school
- someone in your community you would describe as a "character," such as the mail carrier who likes to chat, the Little League coach with the red face, the beloved parish priest who left the church to get married, the neighborhood busybody.

Then I have them take a few more minutes to list as many specific details about that character they can call up. Once they have their own lists in front of them, we discuss the downside of these wonderfully revealing details: they have to be managed. If one or two students share their lists of details, the class can readily devise a means to organize them. Details about the neighborhood busybody can, for example, be divided as follows: physical description, location of his house on the street, his tactics in garnering gossip, specific incidents.

Beyond paragraph organization, the in-class portion of this assignment is also useful in demonstrating unity of purpose. Before I send my students off to actually begin writing their essays, I return to "Ex-Basketball Player." I point out that the underpinning of all good writing—fiction, poetry, expository writing—is unity of purpose. Updike's title is the point beyond which most folks in Flick's town probably don't venture: "Flick is an ex-basketball player"—enough said. But the writer takes a closer look, gathers details, and presents them with a purpose: to reveal what it means that Flick is an ex-basketball player: he is an ex-basketball player and he'll never be anything else.

I have a tendency to wax poetic about that strong relationship between writer and audience which flourishes wherever unity of purpose prevails, so it is just as well I've about run out of class time when I get to this point. I suggest my students try to determine for themselves the purpose of their essay by writing a one-line "thesis" caption to go with the mental picture of the character they've chosen to write about. The purpose may be, for example, to reveal that "Mr. Jones, the neighborhood busybody, is a real pain in the neck," or it may be to reveal that "Mr. Jones, the neighborhood busybody, retired too soon," or that "Mr. Jones, the neighborhood busybody, is a lonely old man." Whatever that caption may be, it will determine not only which details are chosen, but also the order in which they are presented, and the tone of voice the reader ultimately hears.

The Specific Gravity
of Words: Writing About
Richard Wilbur's "The Writer"

~~~~~~

David Mason
MOORHEAD STATE UNIVERSITY
MOORHEAD, MINNESOTA

As a child of scientists, I was always aware of the oddity of metaphorical reading. In my thinking, which baffled my parents, nothing was itself; everything figured something else. Marianne Moore's "literalists of the imagination" were creatures I recognized from the moment I met them. Yet Moore could also be a simple literalist, an accurate observer of the world, and it is perhaps too easy for wanderers in imaginary gardens to stray from their literal paths.

Now that I have taught poetry for several years, I can understand my parents' bemusement at their imaginatively wayward son. Indeed, one of my mild frustrations with that species of thinker known as the English major is that he or she is too eager to leap to symbolic interpretations of every poem, failing to see the literal sense, the felt life in lines of verse. I'm not sure how or when it happened, but many of my students assume that poets never mean what they say, that some lofty, abstracted pot o'gold lies at the end of every poem's rainbow. This can be carried to absurd lengths—symbols of Christ or the grim reaper hidden in every leaf, blossom, or bole.

Though I sometimes pretend that poems have no "hidden meanings," I do not wish to deny the importance of symbolic or metaphorical structures. But students can too easily trick themselves into abstraction, expecting professors to praise their intellectuality, before they have enjoyed the pleasurable relation of words to the world. I call this

125

relation "specific gravity," which literally refers to the ratio of a solid or liquid mass to the mass of an equal volume of distilled water at 4 degrees Celsius. My sense of the heft of words is meant to correspond to the world they represent. But diction is not the only problem my students face; there is also the matter of grammar and rhetoric. A complex and passionate poet like William Butler Yeats is, with surprising frequency, coldly syllogistic in the stanzaic outline of his argument. Too frequently I will ask students what he could mean by a given passage, only to discover that, perhaps under the spell of his powerful meters, they have failed to hear the logical sense of a subject, verb, and predicate. When these fundamental derailings take place, the last refuge of inexperienced minds is abstraction; they go symbol hunting and reduce poems to formulaic equations.

If English majors can fall victim to their own symbolic thinking—supercharged trains flying off the rails of the poem—perhaps freshman have it worse. Somehow they have been taught that poetry is always difficult, always symbolic before it is anything else. No wonder they sometimes think it has no relation to the real world!

Metaphors and symbols must make literal sense before their figurative values can be understood. In both class discussion and writing assignments, I will often outlaw hidden meanings: Frost's scythe in "Mowing" is a literal scythe and the poem celebrates real work for its balance of fact and dream. Again, my point is not to pretend language is other than it is, but to let my students feel the world's weight in words before they drown in exaggerated interpretations.

The assignment I have devised for freshman or introductory students emphasizes two things: literal meaning and the transformative value of poetry. My usual procedure is never to assign a particular poem to all of my students; they are always free to find any poem in the book that is attractive to them. I am convinced that their effort to identify these poems for themselves is beneficial. In this case, however, I might choose several poems for specific qualities, especially a balance of literal and figurative meanings. For the sake of clarity, let's say that I have assigned Richard Wilbur's poem "The Writer."

The assignment has two parts. In Part One, students are to write a paraphrase of the poem. I recommend that they break it into sentences and translate the poem into their own prose statements: "My daughter is in her room writing a story, etc." The room is just a room; it is not a symbol for the mind or anything else.

Part Two is an essay stressing the differences between paraphrase and poem. Two of the differences they might assert are Wilbur's figurative language and the accuracy of diction. The "prow of the house" suggests that the child's room, like her mind in the act of creation, voyages to some unknown destination, a metaphor Wilbur extends through three stanzas, then questions in the fourth when he notices that his daughter has paused—his mind lovingly attentive to her typing. The second figure is the "dazed starling" they once saw trapped in the room, in a panic to escape—another metaphor for writing and so much more. These two figures lend the poem its rhetorical structure, but they hardly explain its precision and tenderness. Students should be attentive to the poet's vivid appeals to our senses: "a commotion of typewriter keys / like a chain hauled over a gunwale, " or the way "A stillness greatens." Why "greatens" and not the prosaic "enlarges"? Why should father and daughter try not to "affright" the starling? Why does it "Batter against the brilliance" and not merely against the glass? Why "drop like a glove" and not a light, feathery thing with wings? Simple accuracy of description takes on figurative meaning, suggesting Wilbur's powerful correspondences between matter and spirit. But accuracy comes first.

Attentiveness to literal meaning in a highly figurative poem should help students appreciate the astonishing precision and care with which Wilbur expresses his love. The "starling" becomes his "darling," and like all parents he finds that there is precious little he can do for her on her flight.

This assignment can be modified to emphasize other elements of poetry such as meter or tone. But the point is always the same: to catch students before they run off into the never-never land of abstraction and help them pay close attention to the specific gravity of words.

Why Is It Poetry:
Reading "The Red Wheelbarrow"

Peter Fortunato
ITHACA COLLEGE
ITHACA, NEW YORK

It's remarkable, isn't it, that after almost three-quarters of a century readers have not exhausted their delight and fascination with the workings of William Carlos Williams's "The Red Wheelbarrow." Certainly, much of this brief poem's appeal is its accessibility: simple language arranged somewhat unusually on the page, and content that anyone can see. But you'd expect we might be bored with these sixteen words by now: you'd expect that what isn't already self-apparent has probably been discussed to death.

What typically happens with a poem, or any work of art as well known as this one, is that when it is brought up, discussion moves quickly away from the piece itself to a critical context woven about it. To some extent, that's what the continuity of culture is: the weaving that continues; for example, relating "The Red Wheelbarrow" to Modernism, or Imagism or literature in the American idiom, and so on. I love this poem, however, not because of its abstract "importance": in its particulars, the poem stays fresh for me. It's true that teaching it to new readers helps keep it fresh, but there's more. If poetry is news that stays news, then that red wheelbarrow of Bill Williams keeps delivering it.

How it does what it does is the question I love to pose to myself and my students—who might think on first reading that the simplicity of the content and some cleverness with mechanics are all there is to it. I might need to point out to them that the poem is fundamentally a machinery of words and asks to be read with attention to the line and stanza breaks, that it has a distinct rhythm, which when vocalized is part of its charm. It's true the simplicity is a delight, of course, and many students will readily compare this poem to haiku, if only because of its brevity.

After having assigned a reading of it, the first thing I do in teaching this work is to write it out on the blackboard without its first two lines, and then ask if there is enough left to qualify as a complete poem. This in itself can be an interesting writing assignment or source of classroom discussion. Most students will eventually see that description is not enough to make a poem, nor is typography, because without the opening, "so much depends / upon," we will want to ask, "Well, *what about* that wet, red wheelbarrow and those white chickens? Why should we pay attention to them?"

Indeed, that question is introduced by the opening lines. "What do you think depends upon the things Williams is pointing out? Why is he pointing them out?" I ask my students. I have found they are likely to write or talk about many subjects here, ranging from the joys of a simple, rural life (and nostalgia for it) to all kinds of social and ecological dimensions that might surround the scene. It's amazing how much that red wheelbarrow can carry, and it can be fun to ask a class to particularize through playful, free association what they can imagine loaded into the wheelbarrow.

A few students will probably arrive independently at what I consider to be the most important dimension of the poem, and if they don't bring it up, I will ask, is it just the wheelbarrow and this particular context, or is he writing about a way to apprehend any everyday experience? The fact that the poem directs our attention so completely to such homely things as a red wheelbarrow, white chickens, and rain water is its accomplishment. It deftly "glazes" the ordinary so that it can be perceived as *extraordinary*. (In this way, the poem is most akin to Japanese haiku, though I don't know that Williams himself was interested in that comparison.) The poem is an example of the sort of perceptiveness that can make anything in our lives, even if only for an instant, a complete focus. In my reading of the poem, *everything* depends upon this moment, because it opens into an activity, a way of being alive that is rich beyond limitation. Poetry speak to that richness. I want my students to see that.

And it has so much to do with the first two lines, so much depends upon *them*. That the simple act of calling our attention to a wheelbarrow and chickens opens up into poetry is also quite humourous, I think.

William Carlos Williams's "The Red Wheelbarrow"

~~~~~~

Roy Scheele
DOANE COLLEGE
CRETE, NEBRASKA

Over the years I have found this little masterpiece to be very useful both in literature and composition classes, regardless of whether the subject under discussion is poetry or prose, since the poem provides an easy point of entry into a consideration of the virtues of compression. In addition, discussing the poem often leads students who are not habitual readers of poetry to overturn some of their inhibitions and misconceptions about the art, while usually holding some discovery even for those students who are "into" poetry.

I start by printing the poem on the board, then adding the poet's name beneath and finally adding the title. Those students who have read little or no modern poetry are typically skeptical as to whether the specimen just produced is a poem at all; many of them equate poetry with rhyme and simple narrative, something more along the lines of "Casey at the Bat" or "The Face on the Barroom Floor."

As we begin to discuss the Williams poem I try to draw them out by asking whether it reminds them of anything, what it is like. We talk about the poem's images (wheelbarrow, rain water, chickens) and colors (red and white, yes, but also the colors implied in the prisms of the raindrops, and in the things not named that might be expected to be there: grass, gravel, house or barn or fence nearby, etc.). Someone inevitably compares the poem to a color snapshot, and we discuss the poem's photographic qualities for a while.

I now turn to a consideration of the poem as a flat assertion. What is the "so much," I ask, that "depends upon" this simple array of wheelbarrow, rain water, and chickens? The students normally view the statement as a species of nonsense. The images seem unimportant in themselves; what in the world is the "so much" said to depend upon this little tableau?

Almost without exception the students take "depends upon" not in its literal but in its idiomatic sense, so I suggest that we look at the etymology of the word "depend": from the Latin *de + pendere*, "to hang down," and they see that what literally "depends upon" the red wheelbarrow is the raindrops. If we now put the literal sense beside the idiomatic sense of "relies on," the poem's images constellate into a meaning: the wheelbarrow, rain, and chickens become part of a larger whole. We are in the realm of symbol and metaphor.

At this level of consideration the wheelbarrow can be seen to represent human labor (and the artifice which makes tools useful to that labor). The rain is symbolic of the renewal and sustaining of life, and the chickens of all the things man raises and eats for his own sustenance. Thus the poem can be viewed as a miniature essay on the interconnectedness of all life, human and nonhuman, in nature, and the poem's assertion becomes not an overstatement but an understatement: that "so much" is *everything*—all life depends on the water that nurtures it.

As a final step I like to get the students to think about the poem's form. I point out that it is written in unrhymed syllabic couplets, four of them, each first line having either three or four syllables and each second line, two; this syllabically regular second line, steadily recurring, replaces the regular metrics and rhyme of the traditional couplet. I try to show how each second line sets up an expectation of two syllables, an expectation that the poem continually fulfills, and how this contributes to the poem's playfulness: breaking "depends upon" into two units in the first couplet, "wheelbarrow" into two units in the second, "rainwater" into two units in the third, and separating epithet from noun ("white" from "chickens") in the last couplet. I suggest that, in terms of the poem's form, what "depends upon" the statement of the opening couplet is the succeeding three couplets. Form follows statement, as it were.

If one wishes to pursue the matter of form, I have found Robert Frost's "Dust of Snow" to be excellent for comparison, having the same number of lines and a comparable brilliance of imagery while being written in rhymed quatrains and having a very different tone and rhetorical structure.

The Frivolous Profundity
of Poetic Music

~~~~~~

David J. Rothman
CRESTED BUTTE ACADEMY
CRESTED BUTTE, COLORADO

One of the strange things about literature—and particularly poetry—is the way that questions that seem either pointless or obvious can yield surprisingly fertile results for critical thinking. For if one function of poetry is, as Alexander Pope wrote, to say "What oft was thought, but ne'er so well express'd" then it is the simplest things that often embody the most powerful forces in a poem.

William Butler Yeats's "The Lake Isle of Innisfree" is a mysterious poem in this sense, for while it appears to be just a simple song of longing for peace and quiet, it is filled with little specifics that shimmer with a symbolic power that is difficult to describe. These little things are worth meditating on at length, not only for what they can tell us about the poem, but because they help us to see what the poem is trying to say about an attitude towards life. One way to ask this question more specifically is to wonder why Yeats has written, in the third line of the first stanza, "Nine bean-rows will I have there." Why nine? The number may be irrelevant, and it may have a private or occult significance; but are there other ways to answer this question?

Without worrying too much about the particular number nine, for example, we might ask why Yeats picks any specific number. After all, he does not indicate how many wattles (poles intertwined with twigs, reeds, and branches) he is going to construct in building his cabin—why count bean-rows instead of wattles, or wattle-poles?

Remember that the point of this kind of an essay is not to hunt down the symbolic significance of the number "9," although such information, and the way that Yeats understood it may well be meaningful and helpful in reading the poem. Instead it is to explore why this specificity, this simple detail, is important to Yeats's imagination, at least in this poem. This is one of Yeats's deservedly most famous lyrics, and if we can discover some of the imaginative relations among the many simple words in the poem (go, clay, nine, alone, peace, slow, night, day), we can begin to articulate the feeling that flows from it. In the end, the purpose is to describe how such simple mysterious words like "nine" are just as important in this poem as the more obviously important words like "alone" and "peace."

Writing Exercise for William Butler Yeats's "Leda and the Swan"

~~~~~~

Mark Sanders
COLLEGE OF THE MAINLAND
TEXAS CITY, TEXAS

A BRIEF OVERVIEW

When we think about Yeats's "Leda and the Swan," our curiosity might be teased by his occultism, the automatic script, his gyres, his swan symbolism, or the myth to which the poem alludes. However, we might make the poem more intimately accessible and contemporary if we also view the poem as follows: one of the principles of Yeats's gyres is that the future is dependant upon the present; frequently enough, the bridge between the two makes way for the destruction of longstanding personal, cultural, or societal systems. Status quo is rocked, ceremonies dissolve, and new orders take tyrannical charge—but not without cost.

We do not live insular, private lives. Every act—large or small—produces innumerable effects. Certainly, we do not ascertain readily all the effects, and we sometimes choose or fail to look beyond the immediacy of an act. If we throw a rock into a pond, we take pleasure in the explosion we created; however, we may overlook the remaining subsequent actions: the leaves that ride the waves, the concentric ripples, the splashing and gurgling of water upon the reedy bank. And what of the deep effects? What did we disturb in the muddy depths? What, besides the peace of calm water, did we destroy?

We are taught that we are created in God's image. God is the Creator, and, because we are like God, we create too. Yet how often do we perceive God as Destroyer? In "Leda and the Swan," God transforms into a swan, a creature both beautiful and beastly. When God rapes Leda, his act of willful aggression, his assertion of power, is a god-act. Ironically, the act is resultant from a creative energy that destroys Leda's peace and calm. We are made to wonder, then, about our own place in the world. Leda's world is our world; it is the quiet pond. And someone, perhaps ourselves, is preparing to throw a rock. A god-act is about to happen.

Let us not, however, minimize "Leda and the Swan" as merely a cause-effect poem. In the last two lines, "did she put on his knowledge with his power / Before the indifferent beak could let her drop?" Yeats burdens Leda with a moral dilemma that all humans must share. To be human is to possess knowledge. We claim superiority over all other beasts because we think and know beyond instinct. To be created in God's image is to share not just physical characteristics but to reflect God's knowledge. Since Leda has had intimate contact with God, she should have acquired a greater portion of God's knowledge and power. Mythologically, she has "married" God and is privy to all that God has. If God is omnipotent and can change and create, then Leda—as well as all of us—is able to know and to change and create.

But what does Leda know? How does she choose to handle the burden of knowledge? She must know that passion is not necessarily an unthinking emotion. She must know the miracle that has occurred to her, that God, despite his violence, has shown her favor. Because she possesses God's omnipotence, she must know the outcome of aggression and passion. Metaphorically, what she conceives is "the broken wall, the burning roof and tower / And Agamemnon dead," not the twin daughters who, in their times of passion and aggression, bring these images of destruction to pass. Leda is not just the mother of Helen and Clytemnestra, she is also the mother of the end of a civilization. She knows this. If she possesses God's power to change and to create, as Yeats questions, she faces a tremendous moral crisis. If she is able to change history, to keep her children from their future violence, why does she not? Why does she allow the violence to occur? Perhaps she chooses to worship her daughters rather than see the destruction that will arise from their birth. However, does this blind love constitute misuse of knowledge and power?

TOPICS FOR WRITING

1. What would you do if you were in Leda's place? You have been blessed and cursed with omniscience, and in your godly knowledge you see that a child of yours is going to be responsible for future destruction. A son will climb to the top of a bell tower on a university campus and kill a hundred people with a high-powered rifle. This act will cause chaos and fear on campuses across the country, cost millions in litigation, produce fathomless grief for hundreds, and prompt related acts of violence. A daughter will poison the drinks of our government's leaders at a special fund-raiser, and all will die. The country will fall apart, and nationwide riots will ensue as the worst, filled with "passionate intensity" (Yeats, "The Second Coming"), maneuver for power. Another child will become a genius specializing in nuclear science, but he sells vital information and materials to terrorists who consequently blow up New York, Los Angeles, Tokyo, and Hong Kong. Millions die immediately, and the nuclear fallout and radiation will kill millions more. You see all this and know that without your intervention these events will occur. Just as you have godly knowledge, you also have godly power. You can change things. What will you do? Will you act against your unconditional love for your children or against the sanctity of your world? Explain your position.

2. Leda is not the only human to whom God showed favor. Her case, certainly, is a violent example, but other examples exist in New Testament stories. As described in Luke 1:27-38, the Virgin Mary is impregnated by the Holy Spirit. The visiting angel tells her that the child will be the Son of God and the savior of humanity. Mary has God's wisdom imparted to her, and she seems almost complacent with the knowledge. "I am the Lord's servant," Mary tells the angel. "May it be to me as you have said."

   However, she also understands the sacrifices involved. Prophecies she has heard speak of the Messiah's self-sacrifice for the sins of humankind, and Mary will live to see her own son crucified. If she had power, as we might suppose she did if Leda's example is parallel, she may have found a way to save Jesus from his death while still allowing him to absolve us from our sins. After all, others to whom God had appeared received power to change and to create. For example, in the Old Testament, God tells Noah about the impending destruction of the earth to divest it of evil humanity. In yet another example, God gives Moses the burden of freeing Israel. Both Noah and Moses are given godly powers: Noah creates an ark that will not only hold all species of animals but withstand an earth-destroying storm; Moses parts the Red Sea, makes the heavens rain bread, and causes a variety of plagues to afflict Egypt. In the fifteenth century, God directed Joan of Arc to lead her army against the enemy despite her gender, societal norms, and limited military strength. The Oglala Sioux warrior Crazy Horse had a godly vision, too, enabling him to wage a successful countercampaign against the white cavalry. So long as he complies to vision's dictates, white men's bullets cannot harm him. Factually, the only harm he ever encountered was through the hands of his own people: once, he was shot by a tribe member over a domestic matter; and, when he died at Fort Robinson, Indian guards held him while a white soldier bayoneted him.

Thus, if God remains present among us, either directly or indirectly in visions or dreams, we have access to a greater portion of God's knowledge and power. Sometimes, we are told that we have divine purposes on this earth, that we are called into God's service. Thinking about what you have seen in your own dreams or visions, or remembering what you have heard from the voices in your head (call these the voices of conscience, if you desire), what is your divine purpose in this world? If you have power to complete this purpose or to alter it, will you? How?

3. Let us say you have not been visited by God, that you have no inside, pragmatic knowledge of Leda's dilemma or of the burdens Mary, Noah, Moses, Joan of Arc, or Crazy Horse

carried. However, your turn is coming. Let us say God will visit you, and God will favor you with knowledge and power. Like these other people, you will bear the cost of such knowledge and power, and you will have to sacrifice something valuable because God has favored you. You will lose your freedom, your family, your son or daughter, your respect from others, or your life. You can see the long-range effects, and this sacrifice will benefit many. Will you allow the sacrifice to occur or exercise the power to keep things as they are? If the sacrifice only benefits a few people, will you allow the sacrifice to occur then?

4. If "Leda and the Swan" illustrates how private acts of violence create a wider spread of violence, consider this phenomena in contemporary times. Argue these two points: one, do private acts of violence at home, as in cases of domestic abuse, create larger acts of violence in society?; two, if violence creates greater violence, and each subsequent violent act creates additional violence, how can we ever bring our world to peace?

5. Let us consider the sensuality of the poem. Passion is both frightening and tender, as Yeats suggests through the poem's language. Consider too, the disparity between female and male sensibilities; once the passionate act is completed, the female wonders about the experience while the male is indifferent. Sensual experience does not have to be limited to sexuality, however; any experience that produces both frightening and pleasurable intense feeling is a sensual experience. Write about a number of specific sensual experiences that you have had, and perhaps consider the distinction of how women and men respond to those experiences.

Drama

General Exercise

Creating a Tragic Character

~~~~~~

Mary Piering Hiltbrand
UNIVERSITY OF SOUTHERN COLORADO
PUEBLO, COLORADO

ASSIGNMENT DESCRIPTION

Choose a figure from contemporary life. This person may be someone from the world of entertainment, politics, athletics, performing arts, science, or academia. (No characters from literary works, please.) Write a thorough, well-organized, interesting essay in which you argue that this figure constitutes a tragic hero/heroine. Support any assertions that you make about this person with concrete examples of his or her actions or activities.

This assignment requires that students compose a definition/criteria match essay. I usually suggest that they construct paragraphs around each of the criteria for a tragic hero.

Students often pose the question, "How can I prove that this person is someone of high standing?" to which I respond, for example, "What is their status in the world of professional basketball?" Off they go to the library to look up some sports statistics. Without realizing it, they are performing two important academic skills: research and backing up assertions with proof.

The assignment also often leads to discussions of proximate versus more remote causes to identify what is the real tragic flaw. For

143

example, is the promiscuous behavior of a certain professional athlete his tragic flaw, or is the underlying personality trait that causes that behavior the real flaw? This leads students to see that sometimes we must look further back to locate the real cause of a behavior and that oftentimes certain behaviors are simply symptoms of a bigger problem. (This is certainly a valuable and necessary skill in any discussion of contemporary social problems and thus has applicability to other disciplines.)

The assignment also reveals the importance of definitions. While a rodeo rider who is now paralyzed as a result of a bull-riding accident may be deemed "tragic" by those about him, he probably doesn't meet the criteria of a tragic hero. (This can often be illustrated by pointing out recent high-profile legal cases [sexual harassment and police brutality] whose outcomes have depended upon just such clear application of specific legal criteria.)

Finally, students sometimes ask, "How does this person's behavior affect anyone but himself or herself?" I usually ask the student how he or she feels about this person. Frequently, the student replies that he or she no longer admires the athlete or actor, or whoever. Discussions of possible cause-effect relationships between the tawdry behavior of certain public figures and the pervasive climate of cynicism often ensue, sometimes leading students to decide that the behaviors of contemporary public figures, no matter how remote, may in fact still have some effect on ordinary people.

This assignment leads to lively class discussions whenever I share students' choices for tragic heroes/heroines. The choices are often unexpected and cause us to think about people in ways that we hadn't before. I, for example, have some difficulty in regarding Tonya Harding as a tragic heroine, but as one student commented, "Willy Loman isn't exactly a very attractive guy either!"

Writing Assignments on Plays

Two Questions to Help Community College Students Read Henrik Ibsen's *A Doll's House* and Beth Henley's *Crimes of the Heart*

Karen Locke
LANE COMMUNITY COLLEGE
EUGENE, OREGON

Our literature courses at Lane Community College are writing-intensive. I apply this method by assigning essays, short or long, in addition to exams. I also require a journal that is written primarily out of class; the students may also add or revise entries after class discussion. For the journal, I provide questions that are designed to enhance critical thinking as well as reading, studying, and class discussion; some journal entries may simply be immediate reactions to the play. Depending on my whim in any particular term, the following questions may be used by the students individually for their journals, in small group work before the general discussion begins, or for general discussion. These questions may be assigned individually or as part of a list of several.

1. In what ways does *A Doll's House* seem to apply to life today? Is it in any way dated? Is the play valuable only as it depicts life in the nineteenth century in Norway, or does it still tell us something about life today? Could there be a Nora or a Torvald in the United States today? (The possibilities for this one are

probably obvious: the students immediately offer true-to-life Noras and Torvalds right here in Eugene.)

2. *Crimes of the Heart* is a play about family values. Would Dan Quayle and George Bush agree with this statement? (Note: to begin the discussion, I make sure all students are aware of Quayle's notion of "family values" and his criticism of TV-character and single mother Murphy Brown. The students quickly see that Quayle would disapprove of the McGrath family, but they also understand that the sisters in this family are not just members of a decadent southern family. Some-where in this discussion we make a list of our own ideas of family values.)

I am interested in feminist criticism, and I teach a course titled Images of Women and Men in Literature, which explores the links among social roles, stereotypes, and literary images; *A Doll's House* fits well into this course. I tend to teach *A Doll's House* from the same viewpoint when I use the play in my Introduction to Drama class as well. We talk about Ibsen's statement that the play is not about women's rights but rather is about human rights. We try to determine whether or not there can be any difference between the two. I ask the students to look up three terms: feminist, humanist, and egalitarian. This exercise can be quite enlightening for some students.

We also explore the historical and cultural aspects of the play, which naturally leads to the expected roles of the era and social position of the characters. In this vein, we try to determine whether or not Torvald is a sympathetic character, and we discuss how realistically Nora is portrayed. Students tend to have more sympathy for Nora, of course; but there are those who find her to be so scatterbrained that they doubt her transformation, and these same students sometimes believe Torvald is misunderstood and unduly rejected at the end. A reminder of willing suspension of disbelief and of the convention of larger-than-life character fits in well at this point in the discussion.

I have not used *Crimes of the Heart* in my Images of Women and Men class; for that course (which includes poetry and fiction as well as

146

drama) I choose plays with major characters in clearly defined male and female roles, perhaps oppositional, perhaps stereotypical, or perhaps atypical. I do use *Crimes* in Introduction to Drama; we discuss the growth and strength of the three sisters as related to characterization and the theme of escaping the past and seizing the future, and we discuss the themes of love and family. When using the question listed above, we discuss Chick as well as Lenny, Meg, and Babe.

Argumentative Paper
on *A Doll's House*

~~~~~~

Al Capovilla
BELLA VISTA HIGH SCHOOL
BELLA VISTA, CALIFORNIA

GENERAL INFORMATION

You have been the family lawyer for the Helmers. In fact, you graduated from the same law school as Torvald. You have been a close family friend as long as Doctor Rank has been.

Torvald has come to you with a request. He tells you he wants to continue as bank manager in the small community, but he is fearful of gossip and scandal. Since Nora has left him, he had made up a story that she has simply gone out of town to take care of a sick aunt. He made up this lie to save his reputation.

Now, he wants you to contact Nora and have her come to your office so that he can try one more time to "talk" with her. He wants you to listen and to decide for him whether to file for legal divorce (charging Nora with child neglect and abandonment) or to try one more time for reconciliation by having Nora move back into the house. He will abide by your *written decision*.

You persuade Nora to come to your office. You listen as Nora and Torvald try to "talk" things out.

148

NORA AND TORVALD'S "TALK":

Torvald, you have never seriously communicated with me. You leave me out of decisions. You don't share your office problems with me. . .

I don't think a husband should constantly discuss the office problems with his wife. [You couldn't possibly help me.]*

My father and you, Torvald, have never let me express my opinions. Both of you treated me as a doll. [I've lived by doing tricks for you, Torvald. But that's the way you wanted it. You and Daddy did me a great wrong.]

It's an exaggeration, Nora! [You loved me as a wife should love her husband. It was simply that you didn't have the experience to judge what was the best way of going about things. But do you think I love you any the less for that; just because you don't know how to act on your own responsibility? No, no, you just lean on me, I shall give you all the advice and guidance you need. I wouldn't be a proper man if I didn't find a woman doubly attractive for being so obviously helpless.]

Note: * [indicates lines taken verbatim from play]

Give me a chance, Torvald! [If I'm ever to reach any understanding of myself and the things around me, I must learn to stand alone. That's why I can't stay here with you any longer.] I'm going to lean on my inner self for once!

Inner self? You are going to [leave your home, your husband, and your children? Don't you care what people will say?]

[Listen, Torvald, from what I've heard, when a wife leaves her husband's house as I am doing now, he is absolved by law of all responsibility for her. I can free you from all responsiblility . . . There must be full freedom on both sides.]

Your definition of freedom doesn't fit mine, Nora. [This is outrageous! You are betraying your most sacred duty.] Have you forgotten your marriage duties as a wife and mother! [Surely you are clear about your position in your own home? Haven't you an infallible guide in questions like these? Haven't you your religion?]

Torvald, don't drag religion into this. [I have another duty equally sacred. . . My duty to myself. . . I am an individual, just as much as you are—or at least I'm going to try to be.]

YOUR TASK:

You have heard both sides of the "talk." In a way the format is like an argumentative paper.

Now, it is your task to write a short decision. Use the format of an argumentative paper. You may select words from Nora and Torvald's "talk" and any other significant lines from the play to support your decision paper. Show both sides of the argument.

Conclude your paper with your recommendation. What do you recommend under the circumstances? Legal divorce or a try at reconciliation?

Spatial Imagery in Henrik Ibsen's *A Doll's House;* or, Nora in a Box

~~~~~~

Beverly E. Schneller
MILLERSVILLE UNIVERSITY OF PENNSYLVANIA
MILLERSVILLE, PENNSYLVANIA

One of the more interesting aspects of Henrik Ibsen's drama is his use of spatial imagery. When I teach *A Doll's House,* I focus a large measure of the class discussion on stage movement, props and scenery, and the symbolic uses of space in the play. In the first class period, discussion of the drama is concentrated on the rich opening stage description of the house decorated for Christmas and the several doors that Ibsen mentions as common, of course, to city houses. In particular, there is the door to Torvald's study that serves to symbolically separate him from the family's main rooms, from Nora, and from the life of the house itself. With Helmer in his study for large parts of the play, Ibsen underscores his isolation from his family and the theme of the failure of communication between spouses. As the class continues to discuss *A Doll's House,* we look for images of boxes and doors and other kinds of barriers that divide the characters. We also watch scenes from the Jane Fonda and Claire Bloom videotaped productions and discuss the details of set decoration. At this point, since the students see that the play has been slightly altered for film (especially in the Fonda version wherein a new scene is added at the beginning about Nora and Mrs. Linde's past), I also have the opportunity to discuss the work of the dramaturge.

After we have begun discussion of the play, which takes usually a little more than a week, the students write their first papers on the use of spatial imagery using the final diagram:

Dr. Rank — T. Helmer

Nora Helmer

Mr. Krogstad — Mrs. Linde

I write this on the board and ask them to develop a thesis and discussion around this spatial representation of the characters' relationships to one another. Students who might be familiar with *Hedda Gabler* may note the similarity in character relations between the two plays, as Ibsen also places Hedda in a boxed-in situation that she, of course, cannot escape.

In addition to looking for images of enclosure in *A Doll's House,* we also search the text for images of freedom; students then go on to discuss in small groups their responses to Nora's decision to strike out on her own at the end of the play. I again direct their attention to Ibsen's use of imagery and add to that a concentration on his language, asking students if Ibsen creates different voices for each character. In their second writing assignment of *A Doll's House,* students are asked to compare and contrast the character of Nora with another character from the play focusing on plot lines, dialogue, images which surround them, and their stage movements.

Responses to the spatial relations paper are generally quite thorough and students seem surprised at how many images of enclosure they locate: the doors, the windows, the letters, the letter box (with its lid enclosing the fateful letters), for instance. Some student writers also contrast the squareness of the house with the spinning of Nora in the tarantella to describe her as something like a projectile going through the roof. Usually the students see the confinement of Nora extending through the appearance of the house and its architecture, onto her associations in the play, and into the language itself; for, it is not until the climax of the play that she and Torvald actually communicate, and their communication results in their final separation.

At the end of the drama unit (which also includes the reading of *Oedipus, Othello,* and *Hamlet*) I test the students comprehensively. Among the essay questions I have developed on *A Doll's House* are: If Nora returns, what do you see happening in the Helmer household?; How realistic does the action of the play seem to you, that is, could you see yourself or someone you know experiencing a similar situation?; Would it be possible for *A Doll's House* to occur in any other setting or at any other time?; or, I ask a compare-and-contrast question involving Ibsen's debt to classical drama to Shakespeare in his use of the tragic plot.

Casting *Othello*

~~~~~~

Janet Eber
COUNTY COLLEGE OF MORRIS
RANDOLPH, NEW JERSEY

Shakespeare is surely the most formidable writer students face in our Freshman Composition II course. His language seems so remote from what they normally read that the majority become discouraged and disinterested. The difficulties are compounded with a play like *Othello* because the title character himself seems both distant and unsympathetic. One student, in our first class session on the play, threw up her hands and wailed "Why do we need to read about a jealous nut who murders his silly wife?" I replied that the work was one of the world's great tragedies, then instantly regretted so pat and pompous an answer that could only widen the chasm between the class's perception of the play and my own. "Who *is* he, anyway?" asked a voice in the back row. "You tell me," I challenged, then proceeded to ask the class how they saw Othello: tall or short, lithe or muscular, rugged or soft? Answers came slowly. We moved to Iago. What did he look like? Could they perhaps describe him in terms of a popular contemporary actor? Did Desdemona remind them of a particular actress? Did Emilia? Cassio? Before they knew it they had cast the play guided by the play itself, those very words that had been inaccessible at the beginning of the period. They quoted dialogue, description, defended their choices, disputed the merits of this or that actor. All they had to go on was the play and they soon learned the rewards of close reading. I was little more than a moderator, joining in only when invited, because this was all their call; they were in control.

Some choices were traditional. They insisted an African-American play Othello, so James Earl Jones was their first suggestion.

Even now he gets a number of votes, though in the past couple of years Denzell Washington has become the favorite. Actors ranging from Michael Keaton to Danny DeVito have been cast as Iago. By the character's own admission he lacks "beauty," and the students examine his soliloquies carefully before they make a final choice. Someone once suggested Richard Gere, but in one voice the class voted him down; "too pretty," they said. He'd make a better Cassio.

Desdemona is harder to cast. Does she really need to be blonde, as she is often traditionally portrayed? Not according to some students who see Julia Roberts's strength and vulnerability as crucial to the role. Even Emilia inspires discussion, the most novel suggestion (pretty well substantiated, actually) being Cher.

The real point here is that students must make all recommendations based solely on the text and their own interpretations. I guide but do not impose my thoughts on them. The exercise is also fairly short, taking about a half hour. I've used it for years now and always with success. It breaks down that wall of resistance students often erect to protect themselves from great literature and also initiates a lively dialogue from which all benefit.

Virtue in *Othello*

Allen Ramsey
CENTRAL MISSOURI STATE UNIVERSITY
WARRENSBURG, MISSOURI

Othello is an excellent literature choice for generating freshman compositions because its plot is familiar and direct. Students understand the play's thematic thrust: jealously is self evident. The challenge is in expanding understanding to the less evident themes and plot devices. Lectures on Renaissance milieu can fill in some of the void, but these sessions quickly pall, and they do not do much to enhance perceptive essays. An approach that I have taken is a brief exploration of virtue and vice in the play, which leads to essay topics related to human virtues and vices. This assignment can be condensed and improvised, but I will describe the topics as I have used them at one time or another.

Perhaps because of relative ethics, we seem to be losing the sense of what the virtues are. Some brainstorming is possible, listing them on the chalkboard. I have also cited the twelve Aristotelian virtues as a matter of expediency. In either case, temperance (the mean between either extreme, "the golden mean") and magnanimity (the combination of the other eleven virtues), are valuable concepts to introduce early.

A virtue that students normally overlook in preliminary discussion is *self-control,* an idea that must be introduced by the instructor. This topic can open new insights about the play and give some direction to character analysis.

Self-control is a virtue attributable to civilization. It is a trait that allegedly sets people above the animals, giving them the control to eat enough but not too much, to compete, but to win and lose gracefully, to dress tastefully, not like a fop. Self-control is so important that civilized society has established numerous conventions surrounding the virtue.

Courting is an example. It requires a man to restrain his urges until a series of conventions are completed—introductions, public exposure, proposal, and so forth. (Cf. Juliet's reaction from the balcony: "I have no joy of this contract to-night, / It is too rash, too unadvis'd, too sudden" 2.2.117-18). Control is proper to gentle people and requires the privileged classes to be a model for the underprivileged.

The irony (and interest) of this topic is in the specter Iago presents. Iago is a model of self-control so that virtue is turned on its head. He reasons his way through a plan to destroy Othello, and he patiently waits for the right moment to strike. He comes from Venice, where wit easily gives way to deceit. Italy is the land of Machiavelli. The jarring point in this play, then, is that the person who possesses the virtue of self control is the villain. Iago's villainy is unnerving partly because we can easily see ourselves in him. As we strive to be sophisticated, suave, or mature, we gain cunning in methods of exploiting others.

The opposite of self-control is impulsivity, a term that brings to mind the character of Othello. Othello is the magnanimous person. He is controlled and generous as he faces down Brabantio in court and explains that he did indeed court Desdemona, albeit secretly. Desdemona loves him for his worldliness, but a kind of worldliness that contrasts with that of Iago. The two characters portray similar traits, but their actions make the rules of society a formula for tragedy. In a handout the principals sort out as follows:

SELF CONTROL VS. IMPULSIVITY

Othello the Moor	Iago the Italian
Wordly—as a soldier	Worldly as a city person
Self controlled— as a military man	Self controlled as a schemer
Implusive in matters of love	Cynical in matters of love
Virtuous in being naive ("primitive")	Evil in being sophisticated
Evil in being impulsive	Evil in being self controlled

[I have worked through parts of this approach at various times in order to deal with primitivism, the term that I think best explains Othello's condition. Primitivism is a virtue—because those who have not been corrupted by civilization retain the purity they are born with. Othello is virtuous in being primitive. The term resonates with meaning today, with our interest in our respective ethnic background. If we can appreciate a simpler, purer past, we may learn something about what our civilization is doing to us today. Yet, we should be aware that returning to our past can permit the prejudice of others to destroy us.]

This review of virtue offers several choices for writing assignments. If one were to teach *Hamlet*, too, Hamlet's urgent desire to be impulsive, but his maturity to be self-controlled, provides some material for a compare/contrast assignment (I have never done this). With *Othello*, the virtues can spin off of the play (fidelity/infidelity; honesty; jealousy; self-control; compassion; fair play; honor). Renaissance values can be contrasted with our own (pride; modesty; worldliness; chastity; submissiveness to one's husband). Or, these traits can be considered subjectively as topics for analysis or as sources of expressive writing.

Cruising with Woody Allen,
or Writing Assignment #7,896,909

Louis Phillips
SCHOOL OF VISUAL ARTS
NEW YORK CITY

> "Sports to me is like music. It's completely satisfying. There were times I would sit at a game with the old Knicks and think to myself in the fourth quarter, this is everything the theatre should be and isn't. There's an outcome that's unpredictable. The audience is not ahead of the dramatists. The drama is ahead of the audience..."
>
> —*Woody Allen*
> *The New Yorker, (June 6, 1994)*

Sure, we could go on forever writing and rewriting the same old themes—e.g. , comparing and contrasting old man Oedipus with foolish man Samson in the Book of Judges (they both have lives influenced by riddles, both have terrible tempers, both have sexual relations with the wrong woman, both end up blind in order to see the necessary tragic content of life, both die in exile), but suppose for now we take another tack (using tact) and concentrate a bit upon the structure of some of the plays included in this collection. Let's cruise with Woody Allen.

Given the choice, most persons on any given night would rather watch a sports event than a play (if you don't believe me compare Public Television's *American Playhouse* ratings with the ratings for any major basketball, football, or baseball game). Why are sports more compelling then plays? Or are they? Do we root for Nora to walk out and slam the door the same way we root for our favorite team to win a game?

Do you agree or disagree with Woody Allen's notions about theater? For example, he believes basketball to be superior drama because the outcome is unpredictable. Think about the plays you have studied. How predictable were the outcomes? Could it not be true that one of the elements of drama is predictability—the inevitability of the outcome? How soon in reading *Oedipus Rex*, for example, do you know that Oedipus has murdered his father and has married his mother? Isn't the outcome of that play certain in the audience's mind long before the drama is played out? Greek audiences of course, knew the stories before they ever entered the tragic festivals, but does such knowledge, not altogether forbidden, destroy the "fun" of theater- going or play reading? Isn't it obvious that Othello's jealousy is going to destroy his marriage?

Are surprise endings better drama than non-surprise endings? Oedipus goes off stage and blinds himself. Were you surprised? Was the dramatist ahead of you? Were you surprised that Hamlet died?

What does Woody Allen mean by the notion of the audience being ahead of the dramatist or the dramatist being ahead of the audience? Apply that notion to any play you have read. In *Hamlet*, how far ahead of us is Shakespeare? How did the playwright get so far ahead?

And, while we are lobbing questions for themes about, like so many life-consuming hand grenades, why not consider the repeatability of plays? Think how many times you could see or read *Hamlet, Death of a Salesman*, or *Oedipus the King*. How many times do we reread a mystery—a literary form whose endings most often depend upon a surprise? How many times will a sports fan sit through the replay of a contest whose ending is already known? Perhaps, true drama transcends the idea of an ending. Perhaps, true drama echoes, not on the bare stage or the hardwood floor, but in our heads—is that not true for sports as well?

EXTRA CREDIT

Imagine a society that preferred theater to sporting events. Would it be a "better" society than the one we are living in now? Why does Woody Allen persist in creating movies?

Appendix:
A Model Course Outline

Some Writing Projects
for Literature Class

~~~~~~

Kathleen DeGrave
PITTSBURG STATE UNIVERSITY
PITTSBURG, KANSAS

In my literature classes I assign many different kinds of writing. Many of the assignments students write in class, to help them learn the material and focus on certain elements of the genre we are concentrating on. But I also give outside assignments, formal and informal. The formal assignments consist of two- to three-page typewritten papers. The informal assignment is a Response Notebook. I describe each in detail below.

GENERAL RULES FOR WRITING ESSAYS

I have my students write essays of two to three pages on specific stories, poems, and plays after we have discussed the elements of the respective genre and studied several pieces closely in class. Since one way to learn to write about literature is to see what other students have done, I have students bring a rough draft of the essay to class and work in peer groups. It always helps if I can show a model of the kind of essay I am looking for on the overhead first. The students bring at least one photocopy of their

162

rough drafts with them so that everyone in the group of three or four can read along as they deal with one paper at a time. I stress the difference between interpretation and plot summary and remind them that quotations should be short so that interpretations of the quotations can be full.

WRITING ASSIGNMENTS FOR SPECIFIC STORIES

"A & P"

Explain what Sammy in "A & P" is rejecting when he says "I quit." Think about what the store and Lengel stand for from Sammy's point of view and what his new relationship to the "hard" world will be.

What is Sammy's attitude toward women? He quits his job, he says, because he wants to look like a hero in Queenie's eyes. Is he egalitarian, defending the young women's right to dress as they please, or is he sexist?

"THE JILTING OF GRANNY WEATHERALL"

Granny Weatherall has a spiritual crisis the first time she is jilted. Why is she able to stand up so well to what she perceives as her second jilting? What has she learned? What *is* the second jilting?

What are the crisis and climax in "The Jilting of Granny Weatherall"? Argue that a particular moment is the moment after which there is no going back, and that another moment is the high point. Be sure to focus on Granny's death as the story, not on her memories; the memories shape her death, but I don't want the crisis of her past—give the crisis of the present.

"EVERYDAY USE"

The quilt in "Everyday Use" plays a symbolic role in several ways. Explain how the quilt functions as a symbol, both in itself and in how it partakes in the action of the story.

The mother in "Everyday Use" has an epiphany near the end. Describe the epiphany and show how it is both the crisis and the climax of the story. What brings the epiphany on? What is the result of it?

"BARN BURNING"

Why does Abner Snopes burn barns? Is he a hero? An anti-hero? Be sure to explain the class system involved in being a tenant farmer.

At what point does Sarty decide to betray his father? Argue that this point is the crisis of the story. *Why* does Sarty betray him?

WRITING ASSIGNMENTS FOR SPECIFIC POEMS

GENERAL ASSIGNMENT

Write a letter to a friend in which you explain why you like a particular poem. Pretend that you have sent a copy of the poem to your friend and that your friend has read it. You will need to interpret the poem for your friend and explain some of the more difficult images and metaphors. But your main purpose is to tell your friend why you would really like him or her to read *that* poem.

"FACING IT," "DEATH OF A BALL TURRET GUNNER," AND "DULCE ET DECORUM EST"

Pretend that Yusef Komunyakaa, Randall Jarrell, and Wilfred Owen were able to meet and talk. What would they say to each other about the meaning of war? Remember that each poet experienced a different war (Vietnam, World War II, World War I). Use word choices, images, and metaphors/similes from each poem to make your point.

"IN MEMORIAM JOHN COLTRANE"

This is a poem about a great jazz saxophone player. Argue that the poem recreates a sense of jazz by its use of sounds and rhythms. In particular, talk about all the sound connections you see (alliteration, assonance, consonance, exact rhyme, slant rhyme) and try to describe the sound and rhythm effects.

"MY PAPA'S WALTZ"

Some people argue that "My Papa's Waltz" is about an abusive relationship between a father and son. Some people say the poem is just about a rollicking, friendly dance—about love. What do *you* think the poem is about? Is this an abusive family relationship? Is it a loving one? Could it be love/hate? Analyze imagery, sound relationships (including rhyme), and rhythm in order to make your case.

WRITING ASSIGNMENTS FOR SPECIFIC PLAYS

TRIFLES

Show how props are used symbolically in *Trifles*. Explain the use of the prop and what the prop symbolizes in each case. Look at all of the props and try to group them somehow. (For example, you could find symbols of Minnie's emotional battering, symbols of Minnie's hard work, symbols of the women's growing comprehension.)

Pretend that you are the prosecuting attorney and argue that Minnie Wright murdered her husband. Show that she had the opportunity, means, and motivation.

OR

Pretend you are the defense attorney, faced with the evidence Mrs. Hale and Mrs. Peters discovered. Argue that there are extenuating circumstances in the case and that therefore the judge should be lenient in his sentencing. Put yourself into the time period of the play as you discuss Minnie Wright's alternatives. Remember that in the era the play is written, the judge and jury will all be men.

A DOLL'S HOUSE

Decide what the moment of recognition and reversal is in *A Doll's House*. What does Nora recognize and how is her situation at the end of the play reversed from the beginning? Show how the action leads up to this moment (or these separate moments if they are not the same) and explain why the dénouement is then inevitable. Use specific quotes.

Many people were outraged that Nora would leave her husband and children at the end of *A Doll's House*. In fact, some versions of the play have her going into the children's room at the last minute and deciding to stay. Which ending do you think is the better one and why? Be sure to refer to the main themes of the play and to keep in mind Nora's and Torvald's characters.

OEDIPUS THE KING

In *Oedipus the King,* trace the successive changes in the attitude of the chorus towards Oedipus and towards the gods, since Oedipus comes into conflict with the gods as the play proceeds. Look at each choral section and decide what the attitude is in each. In some sections, the chorus might focus on just Oedipus or just the gods; in some the chorus talks about both. Decide whether the respective attitudes change, and if so, how. Use quotations from the choral sections to argue your case.

THE GLASS MENAGERIE

Argue that Laura is or is not a dynamic character. Show when and how she changes, if she does. Do not speculate on what she will do after the play. Simply describe her character at various stages of the play, *always* using evidence from the text.

Discuss the ambiguity of Tom's leaving. Show how it is both necessary and cruel—how to escape his "coffin" he has to "drive out at least one nail." What will be the effect of his leaving on Laura and Amanda (not speculation, but using evidence from the text)? Why is it necessary nonetheless that he leave?

Explain Jim's intentions. Why does he talk to Laura about her "inferiority complex" and dance with her and kiss her? Is he being kind? Is he trying to help her? Is he being self-centered? Is he an insensitive lout? Perhaps he has a complex mixture of intent.

Whom is this play about? Which character—Tom, Laura, or Amanda—is the protagonist? Decide what the "center" of the play is for that person, and interpret the plot in light of that person's development. Also, given this protagonist, who or what is the antagonist?

Laura Wingfield is "crippled." Discuss several speeches or dialogues that show *how* Laura is crippled (in what ways, physically, emotionally, socially, she is crippled) and *what* she is crippled by.

Consider the various coats in the play to be symbolic. Discuss the symbolism of each scene in which a coat plays an important role.

JOURNALS

A regular assignment that I make as I teach the three genres is a journal, although the form differs for each.

FOR FICTION, the journal assignment looks like this:

Write from one to three pages on four stories of your choice (from those we are reading this semester). For each story, give three kinds of response: a personal response, a social issues response, and a literary comparison. I want you to engage the story personally and intelligently. Do not summarize the story—we will do that in class. Rather, *react to* the story; make it your own. This is a place to take risks. I will not grade the response notebook on grammar or form, only on your willingness to use your thoughts and emotions as you read.

PERSONAL RESPONSE

Relate the story or parts of the story to an experience you have had, to people you have met. If you have a strong emotional reaction to the action or to a character, explain *why* you have that reaction. It might be just a phrase or a part of the setting that affects you. Let the story mean something personal to you. (Caution: if the story is *too* personal, don't write on that one.)

SOCIAL RESPONSE

Relate the story to a larger social or philosophical issue, like problems of race, gender, class, age, religion, or problems in government, education, law—whatever.

LITERARY COMPARISON

After you have read all four stories, see if you can find some comparisons or contrasts among them. Are themes similar? Do settings seem to repeat? Might some character from one story help you understand the characters from another? What light might one story shed on another? Let the stories interact, have a dialogue in your mind, rather than sit separately in little compartments.

FOR POETRY, the journal assignment is a bit different:

The poetry response notebook will have two parts. For the first part, write an emotional response to any four of the poems we read. Choose poems that you really like or some that make you very angry or depressed. Think about the lines in the poem, the sounds and the images, that affect you and explain why they do. I'm not asking that you talk about yourself, but about the poem and what it does to you, although sometimes it is easier to explain what the poem does by describing the images or experiences it calls up. Reading poetry is most enjoyable when you put some of yourself into it, even if you don't understand the entire poem on your own.

For the second part, write a poem. You might try imitating one of the poems you write about for part one. Or you might write a poem about an experience that one of the poems recalls for you. In the poem, try to use the poetic elements we discuss. Use *concrete images,* not just abstract language. Use unusual comparisons—*metaphors* and *similes.* Use *sounds* to connect ideas and heighten them. Try very hard to make your poem *not* rhyme.

FOR DRAMA, the journal is very simple:

Keep a journal of entries on the plays that we both see and read. Write a page or two on each play, discussing the differences you notice between the written play and the play as it is performed. Always talk about how the differences affect you and affect the theme and characters. Decide which version you like better. Keep in mind what you gain from stage directions on the one hand and from seeing an actor or actress interpret a part and a director interpret a play on the other. Discuss the effect of costumes, stage effects like lighting and music, entrances and exits, blocking, and interpretation of specific lines or scenes.

Index of Authors
And Titles

To The Instructor:

Teaching Composition with Literature is a new book that can greatly profit from the reactions of instructors who use it. Would you be willing to share your opinions on the book and its contents? The editor is also especially interested to hear from instructors who want to share their own classroom ideas for teaching these works.

Please complete this questionnaire and return it to: English Literature Acquisitions Editor, HarperCollins Publishers, College Division, 10 East 53rd St., New York, NY 10022-5299.

Name _____

Position_____

School _____

Address_____

What selections in this book did you find particularly useful?

_____

_____

_____

What selections did you find less useful?

_____

_____

_____

Did you try any of these exercises or assignments in your classes? If so, how did they work?

_____

_____

_____

Do you have any favorite exercises or assignments you would like to share with other professors in the next edition of *Teaching Composition With Literature*? Please summarize.

_____

_____

_____

_____

_____

Would you be willing to write up this exercise for a new expanded edition of *Teaching Composition With Literature*?

_____

If you have any other comments or ideas for the next edition of *Teaching Composition With Literature*, please share them with us.

_____

_____

_____

The Students's Textbook:

Have you taught any poems, stories, or plays that are not currently in *Literature: An Introduction to Fiction, Poetry, and Drama,* that you would find especially helpful to appear in a future edition of the textbook?

_____

_____

_____